SISKIYOU COUNTY LIBRARY

3 2871 00315525 2

DISCARDED

D0602167

SISKIYOU COUNTY LIBRARY

3 2871 00315525 2

DISCARDED

John Scheeler

BIRD CARVER

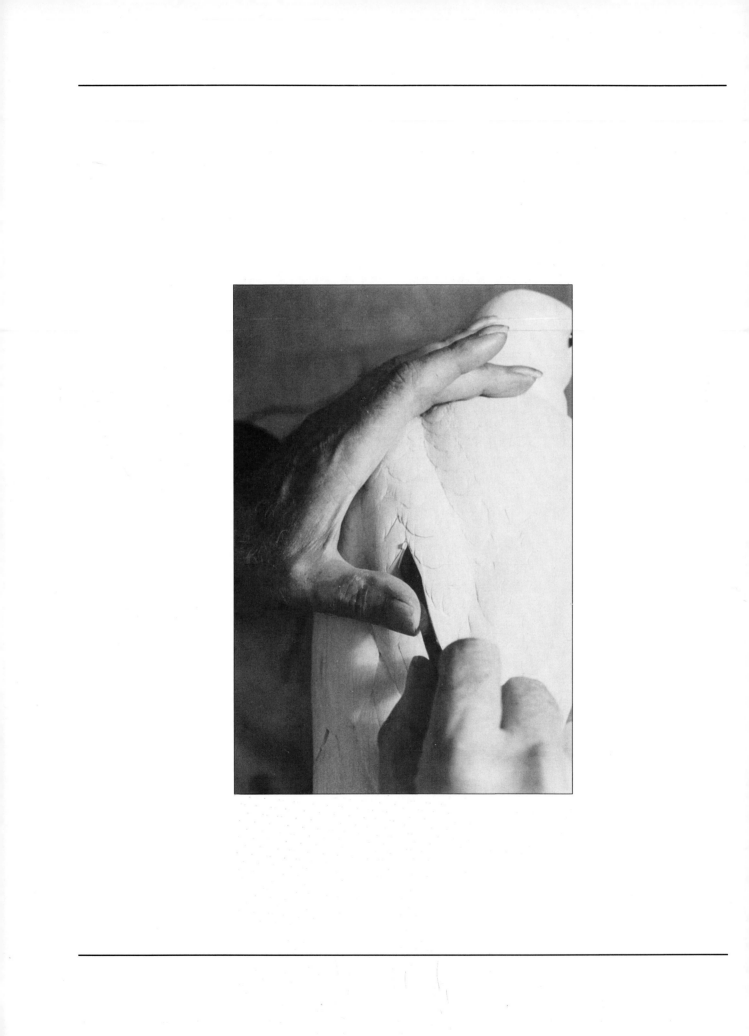

John Scheeler

BIRD CARVER

q
73092
252

Roger Schroeder

Stackpole Books

SISKIYOU COUNTY PUBLIC LIBRARY
719 FOURTH STREET
YREKA, CALIFORNIA 96097

Copyright © 1988 by Stackpole Books

Published by
STACKPOLE BOOKS
Cameron and Kelker Streets
P.O. Box 1831
Harrisburg, PA 17105

All rights reserved, including the right to reproduce this book or
portions thereof in any form or by any means, electronic or mechanical,
including photocopying, recording, or by any information storage and
retrieval system, without permission in writing from the publisher.
All inquiries should be addressed to Stackpole Books, Cameron and
Kelker Streets, P.O. Box 1831, Harrisburg, Pennsylvania 17105.

Printed in the United States of America

10   9   8   7   6   5   4   3   2   1

Library of Congress Cataloging-in-Publication Data

Schroeder, Roger.
    John Scheeler, bird carver / Roger Schroeder.
      p.   cm.
    ISBN 0-8117-1660-0
    1. Wood-carving—Technique.   2. Scheeler, John.   3. Wood-carvers—
United States—Biography.   4. Birds in art.   I. Title.
TT199.7.S394   1988
730′.92′4—dc19
[B]   88-12192
                                                                                 CIP

To John and Edythe Scheeler;
to their children, John S., Harry,
Edward, Denise, Darlene, and Bryan;
and to the patrons, Douglas Miller and Andy Andrews

Editor's Note

Roger Schroeder began working on this book with John Scheeler in 1986. Their collaboration was to have resulted in another volume in the Stackpole series on world-class masters. In midproject, John Scheeler died. Roger Schroeder continued to work on the book, and, with the help of those who knew Scheeler best—his family, friends, patrons, students, and fellow carvers—he has produced a book to help keep John Scheeler's spirit and artistry alive. We at Stackpole and author Roger Schroeder would like to thank all of you who have helped make this book possible.

Acknowledgments

Special thanks and gratitude go to a number of people who helped make the book possible. Edythe Scheeler gave her support to finish the project as did Andy Andrews, who also supplied some much-needed transparencies. Douglas Miller opened his museum, Wildlife World, to me, where I was helped by Miller's parents, Bill and Jan Miller, and by Bobby Nelson. The Ward Foundation allowed me to photograph its collection of bird carvings and gave permission to reprint an excellent article on Scheeler. Byron Cheever also granted permission to reprint an article he wrote on the "New Jersey new-comer" for *North American Decoys* magazine. And he allowed me to add to this book two rare photos of Gilbert Maggioni's work. Ken Edwards of *Breakthrough* magazine supplied three excellent color separations of Scheeler's work. Joe Simeone helped me with photo captions at a point where I thought there was nothing left to write. And, of course, thanks are extended to those people who knew John and were interviewed for the second part of this book.

PART ONE

History

N O   O N E   C A N   P I N P O I N T   T H E   D A T E   W H E N   A   B I R D carver named John Scheeler shaped his first bird. Some who knew him say it was the year 1950. The carving would have been a duck, in any event, for he was a hunter of wildfowl and followed a tradition that was at least 250 years old: He used decoys. And though these artificial ducks had been fashioned from wood, cork, papier-mâché, plastic, and even canvas, all designed to float on water, Scheeler preferred wood for his waterfowl.

Most of the hunting chronicles have described a waterman or bayman who spent his spare time shaping decoys for the hunting season. They were not meant to be true replicas, with plumage finely rendered and feathers delicately raised from the body. They were created to survive transportation, exposure to water for great lengths of time, and gunshot. The finished product, shaped like a duck or a shorebird (before treaties protected shorebirds), had an abstract quality that could fool a bird from a distance. The better decoy makers crafted birds that stood out because of their anatomical accuracy and their bold paint jobs. These carvers were able to capture the essence of the species.

Not surprisingly, styles became regional, influenced by how decoys were to be transported and where and how they were used. The facsimiles became flat bottomed and rounded, keeled and anchored, hollowed and left solid. A fast-river decoy might be streamlined, a bay decoy flat bottomed. Nineteenth-century facsimiles might have had a root head for durability or a bill of a harder material than the rest of the bird.

Some carvers went to great lengths to excel at the craft of carving. Some even sold their birds to be used for decoration. The names Joseph Lincoln, Ira Hudson, Harold Haertel, and Shang Wheeler dominate the annals of decorative decoy making. But three names stand above the rest.

It is almost impossible to discuss decoys without mentioning Elmer Crowell. Born in 1862, Crowell was a witty and intelligent man from East Harwich, Massachusetts, who hunted birds for the metropolitan markets and also worked as a sportsman's guide. From making decoys of ducks and shorebirds, Crowell turned to ornamental birds, many miniature, others full size.

He was a prolific carver. Yet despite the number of birds he produced, some species or poses are rarer than others. A pintail drake he carved around 1915 sold at an auction in 1986 for $319,000, the highest price ever paid for a carved bird.

Crowell shaped birds from the time he was ten until nearly his final year, in 1951. His death probably went unnoticed by Scheeler, who was painting buildings for a living at the time. But the two other decoy makers who helped in the transition of bird craft to bird art did pique Scheeler's interest. He even traveled from his home in Mays Landing, New Jersey, to Crisfield, Maryland, to visit them. Meeting Lemuel and Steve Ward was to have a lasting and inspirational effect on John Scheeler.

The Ward Brothers

They were barbers and baymen who started carving decoys in 1918. Their birds were remarkable for their unique expressions and interesting poses and painted patterns. Some birds were even standing, the pose of most decorative wildfowl made today other than ducks, geese, or swans. The brothers also experimented with insertion, making separate pieces for wings using wood from produce crates. Their styles became their trademarks, and their techniques developed over a span of nearly fifty years while they continued to cut hair into the late 1950s.

As bird carvers got more interested in decorative designs and compositions, birds were not only floated but also posed. These wood ducks, drake and hen, were made in the early 1970s. In the collection of the Wildlife World Museum.

Top *John Scheeler, a pioneer in the field of bird carving, started with simple waterfowl. An early canvasback drake by Scheeler shows his concern for a strong pose that captures the look of the bird. In the collection of the Wildlife World Museum.* Middle *A gadwall from Scheeler's early period, in which he made decoys that were not hunted over but entered in contests. In the collection of the Wildlife World Museum.* Bottom *Note the texture of the head of the shoveler drake and the primaries, which were made as separate pieces and inserted into the back of the duck. In the collection of the Wildlife World Museum.*

Above *A different approach to floating decoratives is this round-bottom black duck by Jim Sprankle, another friend of Scheeler's.* Right *Other carvers followed the Scheeler tradition of strong poses and anatomical accuracy. This black duck was done in 1984 by Scheeler's friend Jett Brunet from Louisiana. In the collection of Richard Stephens.*

In 1976 the Ward brothers were awarded honorary doctoral degrees by Salisbury State College. Governor Harry Hughes of Maryland designated Lem Ward a living treasure in 1979, and in 1981 President Ronald Reagan commended Lem for his contributions.

It was in the late 1960s that Scheeler looked in on the Wards' shop, a simple white building. What he observed or talked about is not remembered. Scheeler was a quiet man but an astute observer. He probably looked at the poses of unfinished and completed birds. He may have asked about painting techniques, which were superbly done by Lem. But the notion that birds could be more than floating abstracts must have had an impact on him. During the following two decades, Scheeler was to become the most recognized carver of decorative birds in North America.

Above left Scheeler's last decorative decoy was done in the mid-1980s. He remained conscious of capturing the essence of the bird he was carving. In the collection of Andy and Sandy Andrews, Jackson, Michigan. Above A close-up of the head. Note how texturing has been refined from that done a decade and a half ago.

An Exhibition in Chestertown, Maryland

It was the prototype of all subsequent carving shows and exhibits. Called the American Bird Carving Exhibit, it was first held at the Parish Emmanuel Church in Chestertown, Maryland. The year was 1965, and it was the first nonregional show of its kind. The program says "more than 200 carvings by over 20 craftsmen from Maine to California" would be in attendance.

There were 24 "craftsmen," to be exact, and Lemuel Ward was one of them. Haertel, who would later be one of the first to judge Scheeler's birds, came from his home in Illinois, another carver from California, two from Maine, and eight from Maryland.

The idea for the exhibit was conceived by Dr. Daniel Gibson, president of Washington College. Gibson was aided by Wendell Gilley, then president of the National Woodcarvers Association, who helped decide who should be invited, and the Maryland Ornithological Society sponsored it. That first program quotes Gibson: "This is probably the most representative exhibition of American bird carvings of this kind ever assembled."

The exhibit became a biennial event: The second exhibition was held in 1967 at the same church and was sponsored by the same ornithological society. One writer reported that nearly 4,000 visitors from twenty states as well as Canada and England came through the church. The number of carvers present went up to thirty-three, and more than 250 carvings of waterfowl, shorebirds, upland gamebirds, and songbirds were on the tables. When it came time for the third biennial exhibit, the show was moved to the fine arts center of Washington College in Chestertown, Maryland. Wildlife paintings were also part of this exhibit.

A carver who encouraged and helped Scheeler with his work is Arnold Melbye of Cape Cod, Massachusetts. Melbye, too, was interested in anatomical accuracy, though he never textured the surface of his wildfowl. He made this black duck in 1961.

Lemuel Ward was at all three events. Scheeler did not attend any of them, for he did not start to carve seriously until 1969. But there was another carver present who would not only inspire Scheeler but would also befriend him.

The Melbye Influence

He was to say of Scheeler's earliest waterfowl that they were the finest he had seen. That was in the early 1970s, and Arnold Melbye had by that time over thirty years of bird carving experience.

This man, who has been described as the dean of American bird carvers, has spent over half his life on Cape Cod. There he visited Elmer Crowell in 1935. Melbye describes Crowell as "the real father of decorative bird carving." Melbye was particularly influenced by

Crowell's miniatures. Indeed, he, too, started carving miniature shorebirds and waterfowl meant for a shelf, not a body of water.

Melbye, who went on to do exquisitely carved and painted songbirds when almost no one was carving them, was also influenced by Wendell Gilley, who helped organize the American Bird Carving Exhibit. It was Gilley who insisted that Melbye start carving full time.

The French expression *trompe l'oeil* means "trick of the eye," or painting nature with such precision that the painted objects can be mistaken for real. This technique is the hallmark of Melbye's birds. For without great detailing, Melbye created feather patterns, softness, and even depth with just paints. It was a method not lost on Scheeler, whose own painting style would make his birds unique.

Melbye worked in virtual isolation. Only at the shows and ex-

Melbye has been called the dean of American bird carvers. His birds are accurate, well posed, and meticulously painted. This is Melbye's marbled godwit. In the collection of the Wildlife World Museum.

hibits that proliferated in the late 1960s and after was he able to meet and influence others like Scheeler.

The 1965 Chestertown show was Melbye's first public exhibit. There he displayed a chickadee, a bobwhite quail, a blue jay with an acorn in its beak, a ruffed grouse, sandpipers, and even some flying ducks. These, though their wings were outstretched, were mounted much as pictures are hung on a wall.

Melbye's flying birds attracted the attention of at least one visitor at the second American Bird Carving Exhibit. This man had been doing what Scheeler was doing: making decoys for hunting. Gilbert Maggioni took in as much as he could, even to counting the numbers of primary and secondary feathers on Melbye's open-winged waterfowl. He was soon to start a revolution in bird carving and would later encourage Scheeler to put his birds into flight.

The Maggioni Years

At the time of the second American Bird Carving Exhibit, Maggioni owned an oyster factory in Beaufort, South Carolina. He still owns the Ocean Lake and River Fish Company. What brought him to Maryland in 1967 was not bird carving but hunting. He came north to shoot ducks and geese. It was on that trip that he decided to go to the Chestertown show.

What he saw there did not inspire him. Maggioni was annoyed. The birds, he said to a friend, were static, actionless. This was not art, he fumed. On the way home, he turned to a young companion and said, "We can do better than that."

Above *In 1973 Gilbert Maggioni of South Carolina finished this peregrine killing a green-winged teal. In the collection of the North American Wildfowl Art Museum, the Ward Foundation, Salisbury, Maryland. Right This composition shows two other ducks escaping the raptor. Scheeler admired this kind of work but preferred to keep his compositions simpler.*

Why did Maggioni consider the Chestertown birds static? The answer was simple. They were not doing what birds do so well—fly.

Flight meant more than hanging birds on a wall. Maggioni thought carved birds should look as if they really were in the air. Hanging them from wires or mounting them on vertical surfaces would destroy that illusion, he argued. His idea was that birds, in their appropriate habitat, could be inconspicuously suspended from reeds or grasses or even simulated water to help create the appearance of flying.

Flight can be described as a cooperation of aerodynamic design and muscle power. Re-creating flying birds, then, requires separating or bringing together feathers on the outstretched wings, depending on the position of the stroke. Doing so, however, created a problem for Maggioni. In a typical wood board the grain runs in one direction. But wings and their separate feathers sometimes run contrary to that grain, resulting in weakened areas on the feathers. The solution, at least to Maggioni, was obvious. He could carve the basic blunt-edged wing from a single piece of wood and attach it to the body of the bird. The feathers could be carved separately and inserted. Supportive habitat and inserts were the beginning of a revolutionary way of presenting flying birds that was to see its finest representations in the carvings of John Scheeler.

Maggioni contributed an impressive body of work. His precedent-breaking flying bird was a wild turkey in flight, which was bought by John Connally, then governor of Texas. Another carving showed two pintail ducks taking off from water, the "splash" consisting of thousands of droplets of resin on aluminum screening.

Maggioni's turkey appeared at the second Salisbury show. Perhaps more important, Maggioni brought a peregrine falcon, one foot planted on a dead widgeon. This style of victorious hawk and vanquished duck was to become one of Scheeler's hallmarks for the next 17 years.

One of Maggioni's most impressive compositions depicts one of those fall days when ducks, pausing in their migratory flights, stop to feed in a marsh or in fields gone to seed. A peregrine falcon has spotted a flock of green-winged teals and picked out a victim. The kill, executed with talons and beak, is swift and in the air. Two other teals are in flight among the tall grasses, but they are safe from attack.

Maggioni's birds are life-size, their wings filled with wooden inserts representing feathers. Falcon and teals are held aloft with steel disguised as stalks and frozen in the moments of death and escape, forever stopped within the confines of a glass case on a small college campus in Salisbury, Maryland.

Salisbury State College is not only a place for students; it also boasts a museum devoted to decoys, hunting memorabilia, and decorative bird carvings.

Maggioni believed that conflicts in nature are the essence of wildlife art. He took this peregrine and widgeon to an early bird carving exhibition. The predator-prey composition was to become one of Scheeler's hallmarks. Courtesy of North American Decoys.

The Ward Foundation

In 1968 the First Annual Atlantic Flyway Waterfowl and Bird Carving Exhibit was held in Salisbury, 60 miles south of Chestertown. Held at the civic center, the show became the World Championship Wildfowl Carving Competition in 1971. During the first three years it was an exhibition, not a place for ribbon taking.

Lem and Steve Ward were honorary chairmen of the show as well as participants. Melbye and Steve Ward whittled a balsa wood

Maggioni was to have a profound impact on the bird carving world as well as on Scheeler. He not only put birds in flight but also made wooden feathers that were separately inserted into wings. Right *Maggioni made this turkey in 1969. Courtesy of North American Decoys.* Above *Another Maggioni piece consists of two pintails taking off from water. The splash is made of resin held together with strands of aluminum screening.*

ribbon at the opening ceremonies. According to the show's souvenir magazine, a prime purpose of the exhibit was to establish "a memorial to Lem and Steve Ward and any other persons deemed to be outstanding in the field of wildlife carvings, wildlife art, and the conservation of natural resources and wildlife, and to perpetuate the memory of such outstanding persons." Other goals were to buy, own, or mortgage real estate to carry out these purposes. What resulted at the hands of local businesspeople was the Ward Brothers Foundation, later known as the Ward Foundation.

It took several years before a home for the growing collection of decoys and memorabilia was found. Finally, at Salisbury State College a large, two-story gallery room with a walkway and railings was given over to the North American Wildlife Art Museum.

Fifty-seven carvers and painters were invited to the 1968 Atlantic Flyway show. Melbye was there, his reputation having been clearly established at the Chestertown exhibits. Harold Haertel, considered one of the best and last of the decoy makers to use his birds to lure ducks, brought strongly posed waterfowl and shorebirds. (William Mackey, in his authoritative book *American Bird Decoys,* wrote that Haertel's attention to detail and species was incomparable.) Others attending who would become well-known carvers and competitors in the 1970s were Robert and Virginia Warfield of New Hampshire; Dan Brown of Maryland; Al Glassford and Robert Kerr, both from Ontario; Oliver Lawson of Maryland; and William Schultz of Wisconsin. These last two had attended each of the three American Bird Carving Exhibits. Both would become close friends of Scheeler's.

The following year, 1969, many of the same carvers and painters attended the Atlantic Flyway Wildfowl Carving Exhibition. During that show some of the most important connections in the history of wildfowl carving were made. Gilbert Maggioni brought his flying turkey. With wings outspread and tail fanned, it is held aloft by a barely visible brass rod, the beginning of the "inconspicuous connection" that keeps flying birds aloft to this day. Scheeler also attended this show. The turkey in flight must have impressed him. But more important to the evolution of carving was what impressed Maggioni. Mounted on a gnarly branch was a stellar jay. Beneath it, blossoms were meticulously recreated from metals glued to small branches projecting from the main limb. This bird was unusual in Salisbury, since these jays are found only in and west of the Rocky Mountains. Also notable were the bird's fanned-out wings and tail. Most remarkable, however, were the feather details, which were not only painted but also burned in. Maggioni was quick to see that greater realism could be achieved with burning. Another revolution in bird carving was about to take hold.

The Minister from New Mexico

Jack Drake, carver of the jay, was born in Thurber, Texas, in 1923. He was one of eight children, the son of a minister in the Church of God. The family moved to Carlsbad, New Mexico, where Drake lives now, and the children trapped animals to help supplement the family income.

During World War II, Drake became a minister himself, later also working as a carpenter and cabinetmaker and carving birds as a hobby. In 1964 he met a bird carver from Arizona named Jack Pence. The meeting was fruitful for both. Pence introduced Drake to basswood for bird carving, the wood preferred by many carvers today. He also gave Drake knives made from straight razors fitted into wooden handles, another device many carvers still use. In turn Drake showed Pence his method of using power tools, such as a band saw and motorized rotary rasp, for cutting and roughing the bird's body. Pence, who was not a bird carver, had also been toying with a soldering iron to put some details into wood. Drake made a startling connection: That same tool could put details on a bird carving.

Another of Drake's contributions to the field of decorative bird carving was the artistry with which he made his habitat. One outstanding piece shows a pair of mockingbirds, one in flight, amid bluebonnets made of painted metal. The feather separations on the outstretched wings are carved with a straight razor blade. The wings, made as separate pieces, were inserted under the natural overlap of the birds' scapulars, which Drake carved on the bodies of the birds. And a small wood-burning iron was used for much of the feather detail. All of these techniques, still used today by most decorative bird carvers, were developed by Drake with little influence from the rest of the bird carving world.

Scheeler was determined to compete almost from the beginning of his bird carving career. This widgeon pair took Best in Show, Decorative, at the 1972 U.S. National Decoy Show, held on Long Island, New York. In the collection of the Wildlife World Museum.

The Early Competitions

While Drake was making mockingbirds, Maggioni getting his birds into the air, and Melbye working on a variety of species, competitions were capturing the serious interest of many carvers. One contest in particular is worthy of note. It is the U.S. National Decoy Show, held each March on Long Island.

The first decoy contest was held in 1923 in Bellport, New York, a small town on the south shore of Long Island. Decoy makers from fourteen states attended. The first prize was $25, in contrast to the $20,000 awarded as first prize for decorative wildfowl by the Ward Foundation. After an absence of some forty years, the decoy contest was brought back to Long Island in 1964 by a group called the Great South Bay Waterfowlers Association. Carvers came from as far away as Canada for the U.S. National Decoy Show, and two Canadians came in first in three of the six divisions, which were divided between professional and amateur classes. Robert Kerr and John Garton would later also be at the first Atlantic Flyway Exhibition.

It was not until 1970 that Scheeler started entering competitions. During the next sixteen years, he would win more Best-in-Show awards than any other carver. But more important, he would win seven of the Ward Foundation's Best-in-World Championships.

Above left *Another carver who influenced Scheeler is the Reverend Jack Drake of New Mexico. Drake was a pioneer in the art of burning in feather detail. He made these scissortail flycatchers in the early 1970s.* Above right *Drake also made these two mockingbirds and bluebonnets. He worked in isolation, and most of the techniques he used, such as putting birds into flight, he developed on his own. Photos courtesy of the Baker Gallery, Lubbock, Texas.*

This goldeneye drake by Scheeler came in third at the first World Championship Wildfowl Carving Competition, an annual event now held in Ocean City, Maryland. In the collection of the Wildlife World Museum.

Competitions are thriving today in other parts of the country, from California to Michigan to Virginia to Louisiana. It was perhaps inevitable that the Ward Foundation, located in a state more noted for its decoy carvers than any other in the union, would start putting ribbons on carvings. The directors of the foundation decided to call its contest the World Championship Wildfowl Carving Competition. The first World Show, as many carvers today call it, was held in 1971. Most consider its ribbons to be the most prestigious.

In the beginning of the World Championships the emphasis was on ducks. At that first competition Julius Iski of New Jersey won Best in World with a pair of oldsquaws. The birds were well posed and meticulously done. Burning had not caught on yet, though Drake's work had been exhibited two years earlier. A Michigan waterfowl carver named Larry Hayden would independently come up with the idea in the early 1970s, and that would propel burning into a national fascination among carvers. Iski was also interested in creating a textured surface on the bird. He had been experimenting with files and V gouges to create feather patterns and separations. His oldsquaws show fine workmanship that stands up to even today's decorative carvings. The texturing had a profound impact on Scheeler, who would later say that Iski was one of the most influential carvers of his career.

There are some remarkable similarities of pose between the pair of widgeons and green-winged teals that Scheeler did in 1971 and Iski's oldsquaws. The three pairs of birds are on logs, in dynamic poses, and with webbed feet, which Scheeler made from copper and canvas. The judges who looked at Scheeler's birds were impressed. At the 1971 U.S. National Decoy Show, the widgeons won Best in Show. They were among the first birds that Scheeler textured.

Left *Scheeler returned to the World Championship of 1972 with a pair of red-breasted mergansers. He took the Best-in-World title, his first. This is the merganser drake. In the collection of Andy and Sandy Andrews.* Below *A close-up of the merganser hen that helped Scheeler win the World title. In the collection of Andy and Sandy Andrews.*

Above *The World Champion-ship Competition has also given World titles to decorative wildfowl other than ducks. Scheeler entered these kestrels in the 1972 World Competition and took the Best-in-World title. In the collection of the Wildlife World Museum.* Above right *A close-up of the lower bird.*

When Scheeler took a pair of goldeneyes to the World Show of 1971, they lost to Iski's oldsquaws. Scheeler was upset. Early on, he made it clear that he did not like losing: He wanted to be recognized as the best. The following year he returned to the World Competition and entered a pair of red-breasted mergansers. They won the Best-in-World title for ducks.

But the show, like its counterparts, was beginning to recognize decorative birds other than waterfowl. The work of men like Maggioni, Melbye, and Drake, none of whom ever entered a competition, was getting as much notice as the decoy. It was inevitable that ribbons be given to gamebirds, songbirds, shorebirds, seabirds, and birds of prey.

Scheeler took a pair of kestrels to Salisbury in 1972. Though almost crude by today's standards, they are open-winged, angry-looking birds perched on a piece of driftwood. They took the Best-in-World title for decorative life-size birds. In the next nine years Scheeler would win five more World titles.

Though Scheeler started with flat-bottomed decoys and continued to make them, his interests turned to other species of birds, particularly predatory ones. Years after he made his kestrels, he

would say of hawks and falcons, "I like the wild look. That's the way I see them." While Maggioni was working on his peregrine and three green-winged teals, Scheeler was working on a peregrine and a single green-winged teal. Instead of hovering in the air, Scheeler's falcon stands with its victim securely under one foot, draped over a crotch in a sizable piece of driftwood. The hawk is posed in a strong upright position, its expression fierce and dominant. Also apparent are the muscles and chesty look of the peregrine. Scheeler had been experimenting with grinding tools to create those effects. He was to start yet another movement that pushed for greater realism in bird carving.

Scheeler's peregrine and teal composition took the 1973 Best-in-World title. The judges, most of whom had been carving passive-looking ducks, did not disapprove of the violence and death suggested by the piece. That made three Best-in-World titles for Scheeler. He was determined to win another.

He went back to New Jersey and decided to try the same theme of predator and prey for the following year. He came up with an Arctic gyrfalcon and oldsquaw. The falcon stands slightly away from the duck, which is dead. Scheeler did not win Best in World in 1974, though he did come in second. A carver named William Koelpin,

When Scheeler moved from waterfowl to such birds as raptors, he continued to be concerned with a strong pose. Above left His peregrine and green-winged teal composition took the Best-in-World title at the 1973 competition. In the collection of the Wildlife World Museum. Above A close-up of the dead green-winged teal.

Above *Scheeler entered this Arctic gyrfalcon and oldsquaw in the World Championship Wildfowl Carving Competition of 1974. It took Second Best in World. In the collection of the Wildlife World Museum.* Above right *The gyrfalcon was another favorite bird of prey.*

who had come in second the year before with a mallard hen and ducklings, entered a white-fronted goose confronting two green-winged teals. Those birds won the title.

Undaunted, Scheeler did not give up on his predator–prey formula. He returned to the World Show in 1975, this time with a prairie falcon and dove. Like the previous entry, the raptor is standing off from the prey, though in this composition the falcon is looking up. The vanquished mourning dove is on its back, unlike the oldsquaw and teal of past displays, and the look of death is memorable. Scheeler added another unusual feature. Though the birds are still on a piece of driftwood, there are cactus segments behind them and rocks under them. Scheeler was now complementing his birds with habitat.

That year the tables turned in Salisbury. William Schultz had brought in a composition of four green-winged teals and sandpipers. Though these teals had obviously been popular with judges in the past, they were not appealing enough to beat Scheeler. He again took Best in World.

That made four titles for Scheeler. Could he do it again? He came back in 1976 with a radical departure for him. The composition shows a long-eared owl taking off from a piece of driftwood. With wings outstretched, it carries a dead mouse in its beak. It was the first time a mammal had been incorporated into this kind of composition. And it was the first time that a bird in flight had won the Best-in-World title.

Top left *One of Scheeler's most successful pieces of the 1970s is this prairie falcon and mourning dove. In the collection of the Wildlife World Museum.* Top right *Scheeler incorporated cactus segments and stones in his piece. Later compositions would minimize the use of habitat.* Above *A profile view of the prairie falcon.*

This long-eared owl and dead mouse earned Scheeler the 1976 Best-in-World title. One of Scheeler's peers, Jim Sprankle, has said that no one could match his ability to capture life and death in avian art. In the collection of the North American Wildfowl Art Museum.

On the Wing

The wings of Scheeler's long-eared owl are fully inserted with feathers. Each of the primaries, secondaries, and coverts was made separately, as were the tail feathers. Over 100 individual pieces had to be carved for the wings, with the barb and quill lines burned and then painted. Many feathers on the body are also inserts.

Scheeler struggled with the issue of inserts for a few years. In 1973, he made his first flying bird. It was a black duck, suspended above the base on a cattail leaf. As with the owl, numerous feathers were inserted into the wings.

He was displeased with the piece. The inserts did not look right to him. Characteristically, he called another carver for advice, a practice he would continue until his death in 1987. This was Maggioni, who responded with a six-page letter, including five illustrations he drew himself. It reads:

> On a partially folded wing (and except on the deepest part of downstroke the wing is partially folded) it will be best to carve basic wing with the outer part at a slightly different pitch from inner wing; but both outer & inner wing still in one piece.
>
> Be sure when inserting primaries that the imaginary continuation of each shaft intersects this imaginary line of the outer wing.
>
> On underwing, be sure underwing primaries overlap secondaries, greater & lesser middle coverts. The outer wing is separate entity from inner wing, folds under inner wing. This is quite obvious but easy as hell to screw up when carving.

These details of Scheeler's long-eared owl show the tremendous number of inserts he did. Insertion is a technique he picked up from Maggioni.

Note—

Slot for greater coverts on upper wing may be eliminated by gluing in the middle coverts after burning them but before painting. These then form upper part of slot for greater coverts.

Main thing is to start slotting with ample thickness of basic wing. Cut main slot first for primaries & secondaries. Wing may then be thinned from top & bottom as desired.

On upper wing you can start anywhere to insert. I've done some with 5 or 6 courses of inserted feathers.

On a duck, this upper wing slotted as indicated will take 10 primary coverts, 10 primaries, 10 secondaries, 5 tertials, 11 greater coverts, 11 middle coverts, 4 alula feathers.

It was a thorough anatomy lesson on wings and feathers, and it was Maggioni's basic approach to achieving greater realism in flying birds.

Scheeler applied much of this advice to the long-eared owl, although he found making individual feathers tremendously time-

Scheeler's first flying bird is this black duck, done in 1973. This was Scheeler's first attempt at feather insertion. In the collection of the Wildlife World Museum.

consuming and tedious. Still, the method produced success: He won Best in World with the owl, so he went home and set to work on a composition for the 1977 World Championship.

Interestingly, Scheeler never got to put a bird of prey other than that owl into the air. No peregrine or prairie falcon ever flew in his studio, though he did put other birds in flight and he was planning on carving a flying sharp-shinned hawk, which never got beyond a clay model. He came back to the World Show of 1977 with a pair of Arctic terns fighting over a fish while in the air. It is undoubtedly his most animated piece. The birds are suspended from marsh grasses. On the base, which is considerably smaller in diameter than the outstretched

Left *A close-up of the black duck.* Below *A close-up of the head shows that the feathers have been slightly raised, another trend toward greater realism in decorative bird carving.*

Above *Scheeler's pair of Arctic terns was entered in the 1977 World Championship and finished second. In the collection of the Wildlife World Museum.* Right *Scheeler did a great number of inserts for these birds, including the tail feathers.*

wings, Scheeler returned to the use of habitat, which he omitted from the owl and mouse piece. On it are oyster shells carved from wood. The judges were impressed with the piece, but not enough to give it Best in World. It came in second, behind an American bittern and a marsh wren in cattails.

A Tradition of Waders and Shorebirds

Until 1918 birds like bitterns and others found in marshes and along beaches could be hunted. They were usually decoyed with stickups that were nothing more than silhouettes of the bird. Scheeler said he liked waders and shorebirds for their colors. But the legs of

Top left *A close-up of the birds shows how one tern helps suspend the other, a difficult pose that required considerable design.* Above *Oyster shells are part of the birds' habitat. He incorporated some shells into a later composition.* Left *Shorebirds were first done as stickup decoys, but soon the plumage and possible poses of both shorebirds and wading birds began to fascinate decorative bird carvers, including Scheeler and Melbye. This is one of several stilted sandpipers Melbye carved. In the collection of the Wildlife World Museum.*

Scheeler was vitally interested in poses that reflected the nature of the bird, and he preferred a strong, upright stance for many of his birds. Above *Though he made few gamebirds, Scheeler did do this scaled quail.* Right *A Virginia rail.*

many of these birds are long and can contribute to interesting poses. In the 1970s Scheeler made a Virginia rail and an American avocet. In the 1980s he made a flying willet, a green heron, a clapper rail, and a pair of ruddy turnstones. He even carved some gamebirds, including doves, a scaled quail, a chukar partridge, ruffed grouse, and a bob-white quail, all done by other decorative carvers over the years. But, as with the raptors, the viewer got the feeling that Scheeler was as much interested in the personality and behavior of the birds as he was in their colors.

William Schultz Remembered

The 1977 Best-in-World bittern and wren composition was also a study of behavior and personality. It was the only World Championship piece done by one of the masters of decorative bird carving, William Schultz.

Schultz, from Wisconsin, was no newcomer to carving. He had been at the three American Bird Carving Exhibitions and the first Atlantic Flyway Exhibition, and he had come in second in the World Championship with his green-winged teal and sandpipers.

The bittern and wren composition has been described as a linear piece, though the cattail blades are bent. Bitterns assume a posture that conceals them in the grasses where they make their homes; the wren, balanced on a cattail stalk, is also common to this environment. The rules of the competition demand that two birds be carved for the World-Class title, though they can be different species and sizes. The wren seems a finishing touch to the story of the bittern.

Born in 1925, Schultz grew up a hunter and decoy carver, having made his first bird out of a discarded cedar washline pole at the age of fourteen. In 1946 he went to work at the Milwaukee Public Museum. He painted museum dioramas and conducted natural history expeditions.

This shorebird is an American avocet carved by Scheeler. In the collection of the Wildlife World Museum. Below The back of the bird. Below left The legs of this bird are made of metal.

For years Schultz made gunning decoys and decorative ducks for competitions as well as shorebirds, gamebirds, and birds of prey. Between 1967 and 1983, the year of his death, he won over 140 first-place awards and 73 runner-up awards. He took both first and second seventeen times.

But more remarkable was the amount of work he was able to produce. In 1974 alone his list of completed birds included seventeen pairs of floating decorative waterfowl, a loon on a nest, a purple gallinule on a lily pad, a pair of black-necked stilts on a nest, a pair of ivory-billed woodpeckers, a pair of Hudsonian godwits, a pair of Carolina parakeets, a jacana on a lily pad, a pair of mandarin ducks, a pair of burrowing owls, one hawk-owl, a pair of Eskimo curlews, a sun bittern, a pair of nonfloating pintails, and a composition of five green-winged teals and two sandpipers that he entered in the World Show of 1975.

Though the jacana can be found in parts of Texas, it is primarily a Central and South American wading bird. Schultz had seen the bird walking on lily pads on one of his expeditions. It was one of many significant contributions he made to the bird carving world. He brought to the public's attention species most people had never seen before.

One of Schultz's final compositions included a bird rarely spotted outside the rain forests of Central and South America. Not unlike Scheeler's predator and prey pieces, the harpy, which has been described as the world's most powerful eagle, stands over a dead red-shouldered macaw. Over three feet tall with wings stretching over four feet, this eagle is probably the largest life-size bird carving ever executed.

The eagle and macaw now stand as the centerpiece of a museum room in Colorado. Much of the work Schultz did from 1973 until he died is there. And so too are forty of Scheeler's works.

The Patrons

The Wildlife World Museum is on a road that runs parallel to Interstate 25 in Colorado. Located in a town called Monument, the museum, which has a 17-foot-long bronze elk in front, has no fewer than 900 bird carvings. Most made in the 1970s, they represent a decade of ingenuity, workmanship, and history.

The museum was founded and is still owned by Douglas Miller. A collector of decoys since the early 1970s, Miller did what no one had done before him in this field. He hired carvers to create birds full time. The results of their productivity during their employment would be his alone.

Miller employed three artists in the early 1970s. One of them was Schultz, who quit his job in 1973 with the Milwaukee Museum

Another of Scheeler's friends and contemporaries was William Schultz of Wisconsin. Schultz was a master of design and composition and introduced unusual birds to the carving world. Done in 1974, this is a jacana on a lily pad. In the collection of the Wildlife World Museum.

to pursue a carving career. Another was William Koelpin, who had been a fire inspector. He went to work for Miller in 1971. The third was John Scheeler, who signed a contract with his patron in 1972.

Scheeler did more than forty pieces for Miller while working from his home in New Jersey. He was able to make his own schedule, working on what he wanted to do: more flying birds as well as gamebirds and shorebirds. Scheeler and the two others could work with the art form in mind, not just produce pieces that would pay the bills.

Scheeler stayed eleven years with Miller, then decided to work for someone else. He was not unhappy with his boss. He said simply he wanted a change. In 1983, the day after his contract with Miller expired, he signed a contract with a businessman from Michigan named Andy Andrews. He stayed with Andrews until his death in 1987.

Above *Scheeler continued to explore the predator–prey theme throughout his carving career. He did this Harris' hawk and dead rabbit in 1978. Entered in the World Championship of 1978, it took Second in World. Scheeler said it was his favorite piece. In the collection of the Wildlife World Museum.* Right *A side view of this bird, which is mantling, a protective posture.*

New Designs for the World

Miller did more than employ carvers. He put up the prize money for the early World-Championship pieces. In 1975, the year Scheeler won with his prairie falcon and dove, the prize for Best in World was $3,000. By 1985 it was $20,000, though Miller had stopped collecting before then.

While working for Miller, Scheeler continued to enter the World Class. In 1978 he entered a Harris' hawk, its wings outspread, clutching a dead rabbit in its talons. Shortly before he died, he said it was his favorite piece. Perhaps he thought it necessary to go back to the predator–prey theme after losing with the terns, though by this time he was thoroughly enjoying doing raptors anyway. The Harris' hawk came in second to a pair of clapper rails fighting over a snail. The

Left *The underside of the hawk's wing.* Below *Scheeler enjoyed making the rabbit as much as he did the hawk.*

Around the time Scheeler entered his terns in the World Show, circular arrangements became popular with wildfowl artists. Below left *This composition of two jungle fowl in conflict was done by Scheeler's friend Lynn Forehand of Virginia. It took Best in World for 1979. In the collection of the North American Wildfowl Art Museum.* Right *Scheeler entered the World Show of 1980 with a circular arrangement of ruffed grouse. It won Best in World for that year.* Below right *Scheeler was interested in capturing the motion of escape with these game-birds.*

piece was done by Anthony Rudisill. And it was Scheeler who got him started in carving birds.

Rudisill had been a wildlife painter specializing in birds, and he lived only fifteen miles from Scheeler in West Atlantic City. Perhaps the friendship that lasted a decade was inevitable.

The judges were impressed by the balance and circularity of Rudisill's rails, which could be viewed from a variety of perspectives. The same circularity was true of Scheeler's Arctic terns, which earlier took a Second in World and may have influenced Rudisill. Another interesting similarity to Scheeler's terns is the oyster shells that complement the clapper rails and seem a natural part of their habitat. It was Rudisill who became a master of incorporating habitat into a piece without detracting from the birds.

Scheeler did not enter a piece in the 1979 World Show. Rudisill entered a pair of green herons fighting over a crab, another circular arrangement that came in Third in World. Best in World was taken by a pair of jungle fowl by Lynn Forehand. Suspended in air, these birds fight beak and talon over a dandelion plant, the seeds of which are scattered by battle. The birds, which have hundreds of inserts, can be viewed from a variety of angles. The circular arrangement had taken a firm hold on bird compositions.

The tail feathers for the grouse were inserted.

An Explosion of Grouse

Two ruffed grouse take off from a forest floor, fall leaves swept up in their hasty departure. Scheeler spent a good part of 1979 creating them. But unlike the Arctic terns or Rudisill's clapper rails or Forehand's jungle fowl, the grouse do not face each other. Their flights are in opposite directions. Scheeler described this piece as an explosion.

The birds are in full flight, wings extended and inserted with separate feathers. The birds are well balanced, their wings in different aerodynamic positions. There is nothing static about this piece. The sensation of flight is almost without equal.

The ruffed grouse won the Best-in-World title for 1980. That made the sixth for Scheeler.

McKoy's Covey Rise

While Scheeler was working on his ruffed grouse composition, a carver in South Carolina was also working on a composition of flying birds. Few carvers were putting birds into the air, and fewer still were tackling more than two birds. Scheeler, of course, had done a pair of grouse, a pair of terns, a single owl, even a pair of green-winged teals on the wing. But never more than two birds. Forehand had successfully gotten three birds into the air. He composed three mourning doves spiraling up from a cornfield along a vertical axis and three Ross' gulls rising above each other from a circle of resinous ocean water confined in a base. And Maggioni had carved four doves flushed from a cornfield. But who could have conceived of putting thirteen birds into flight?

It took Grainger McKoy to do that. When Maggioni, after leaving the second Chestertown show, said, "We can do better," it was McKoy he was speaking to.

After graduating from Clemson University in South Carolina, where he took a degree in biology, McKoy teamed with Maggioni for a two-year apprenticeship–association. In 1972 he made a red-tailed hawk swooping down on a pheasant. That composition is less than twenty feet from Maggioni's peregrine and teals in the North American Wildfowl Museum in Salisbury. Another notable McKoy piece has two red-shouldered hawks fighting over a copperhead snake—in the air. He even has three airborne herons fighting over a fish. Yet another in-the-air composition shows five green-winged teals on the wing.

Five seems to have been the limit on birds in flight. How, then, did McKoy come up with thirteen birds, bobwhite quail in this case, and put them on the wing?

He had been on a bird hunting trip with his brother. Their hunting dogs pointed to an area where the grass was not so thick, and McKoy walked to the place, thinking the dogs had detected only a field rat. It was then that the quail flushed, practically into his face. He decided that day to do a covey rise.

McKoy made some preliminary sketches but ultimately relied on Styrofoam models, much as Scheeler was to do with his ruffed grouse. Styrofoam, as Scheeler learned, is easy to shape, and when cardboard wings are added, it gives an approximation of a bird. This model is especially helpful when deciding on how a bird is to be put into flight and ultimately supported.

McKoy got his Styrofoam quail into flight with chemistry lab clamps and brass tubing that held the clamps at right angles. He could easily position the birds both horizontally and vertically. The whole composition was placed on a turntable so that he didn't have to walk around the project.

What finally held the wooden quail aloft? First, weight was a factor, so McKoy cut each bird body in half, hollowed out the parts, and joined the halves with glue. Then he ran ribbons of annealed knife-blade steel into the birds' cavities. Another length of steel emerged from beneath a wing and ended as a detailed feather. To this steel feather he welded a steel feather of yet another bird. Though two of the thirteen quail are still on the base, McKoy has the highest bird four feet above the lowest birds.

McKoy spent some twenty months on this covey, which was not finished until the spring of 1981.

Another carver who has explored flight is Grainger McKoy of South Carolina. These are five green-winged teals.

A Goshawk and Crow

At almost the same time that McKoy finished his quail sculpture and Schultz was just starting his harpy eagle, Scheeler was completing the piece that would win him his seventh and final Best-in-World title.

He entered a goshawk and crow in the show, which in 1979 had been brought twenty-five miles east of Salisbury to Ocean City, Maryland. The hawk is in a mantling, or protective, position over a dead crow. The pose of the predator, with one foot on the breast of the crow, is dramatic, and the feather insertion is superb. Not only are the tail and wing feathers of the goshawk inserted, but most of the feathering on the crow is also made up of separate pieces.

Scheeler's last World title was won with the goshawk and crow. It was entered in the 1981 World Championship. In the collection of the North American Wildfowl Art Museum.

Many of his peers consider this to be Scheeler's finest piece, and many describe it as the ultimate in what bird carvers can achieve with wood and paint.

Quiet Poses for the World

In 1982 a Canadian named Pat Godin won Best in World with a pair of standing black ducks. The habitat includes water, rocks, small stones, and a muskrat. Not since 1976, when Scheeler put a dead mouse in an owl's beak, had a mammal been used in a winning piece. But in this composition the mammal contributed an element of surprise rather than conflict.

Rudisill took his second World title in 1983 with a pair of black-crowned night-herons. One of the birds is an adult, the other a juvenile. Both are seeking balance on driftwood in a setting of marsh grasses and mussel shells. They do not face each other. In fact, instead of conflict, there is a suggestion of protectiveness. What has come to be called the quiet pose was starting to take hold of the bird carving world.

Scheeler entered a pair of surf scoters that year: alert, dark forms posed on light-colored rocks. They embody what Scheeler insisted on in his final years, the all-importance of form and attitude. But this was the last time he entered birds into World Class.

Pennsylvania carver Ernest Muehlmatt is well-known for quiet poses, the look he believes most birds have immediately prior to encountering a human. There is the beginning look of surprise, though, like Scheeler's birds; they are neither startled nor aggressive. It was with this pose in mind that he carved five bobwhite quail in a

Scheeler thought that the goshawk has the fiercest look of all the birds of prey.

desert setting of cactus plants, sand, a cow's skull, and a tall wooden branch. It won Best in World in 1984.

Scheeler's goshawk and crow composition was not the last World winner to show conflict or death, though the trend was certainly favoring almost benevolent creatures. Larry Barth had been particularly influenced by Scheeler's predator and prey compositions. Barth worked up a piece for the 1985 show that has a snowy owl clutching a bonaparte's gull with one foot. Though there is drift-wood, sand, and grasses, the habitat does not dominate the birds. That habitat should be subordinate to the bird was also one of Scheeler's axioms.

Not mantling, the owl is in a quiet pose, one probably preferred by the judges over Rudisill's mantling red-shouldered hawk and rabbit and Muehlmatt's mantling great horned owl and bobwhite quail.

Maggioni's notion that birds are best displayed in flight would seem to have been displaced by other artistic considerations. Yet Barth returned to the World Show in 1986 with a pair of flying terns, one over the other. The wing of the bottom bird is lightly touching a tall, oblong base with a suggestion of water carved on its top surface. Birds were beginning to look like sculptures, with bases appropriate for sculpture. The carving world was impressed with the composition. Barth took home the Best-in-World title.

High-Tech Tools

Sculpture is a word heard frequently today in the bird carving world. But it took one tool in particular to help with the transition from crude replicas of birds to anatomically accurate ones: the flexible shaft grinding tool known as the Foredom. It was Scheeler, more than any other carver, who helped introduce this device to carvers.

The Foredom has been described as an oversized dental tool. The ⅛-horsepower motor is housed in a canister that can be put out of the way by hanging it on what looks like a stand for intravenous solution. Between that and the handpiece, which comes in different sizes and has prelubricated ball bearings, is a flexible rubber shaft about three feet in length. An accessory used by most carvers is a rheostatic foot control: The more pressure exerted on it, the more torque and the greater the speed. The maximum revolutions per minute (rpm) for a Foredom is 14,000, a speed low enough to accommodate even a sizable barrel-shaped bit.

The Foredom had been developed for the dental industry. Scheeler saw its benefits for carvers in the beginning of the 1970s. Until then, most carvers had used band saws and knives to get the shapes they wanted.

Scheeler never abandoned the Foredom, though he did start to use a tool called the Gesswein. With its origins in the metalworking industry, the Gesswein is a high-tech grinder with a very high rpm: from 10,500 to 45,000 without the optional foot rheostat. Control is achieved with a simple lever on a control box. The handpiece is lighter than those adaptable to the Foredom, but it cannot deal with large steel cutters. Its biggest advantage, however, is that it is controlled through a lamp-wire thin, flexible cord that extends to over six feet. Scheeler would especially praise this tool during the last year of his carving.

The Writers

In a book published in 1972, the Foredom is described as a tool best suited for small detailed work but not powerful enough to remove large amounts of wood quickly. A high-speed grinder that must be held in two hands is recommended instead.

The book is *Game Bird Carving,* by Bruce Burk. Born on a farm in North Dakota in 1917, Burk went to work for Hughes Aircraft in California when he was twenty years old and stayed in California for the rest of his life. Burk worked at Hughes Aircraft as an aeronautical engineer, which had no small impact on this book that sold over 120,000 copies.

Burk decided to do some duck carving in 1954. He ended up making a landing mallard with outstretched wings. Later, he worked on commission doing bird carvings for sporting goods stores.

Burk was invited to participate in all three of the Chestertown exhibits, and pictures of his birds were each show's brochure covers. But the only show he attended was the 1969 exhibit. There he met Wendell Gilley, who suggested to Burk that he do a book on bird carving.

Game Bird Carving is encyclopedic and was perhaps the most important book of its kind for nearly a decade. Although Burk rarely came east, he did dedicate the book to Gilley, to Arnold Melbye, and to the Wards. In the acknowledgments he thanks Gilbert Maggioni and Grainger McKoy for gamebird data.

Throughout the volume there are tables of dimensions, jigs, photos showing how to use tools, even patterns with grid overlays, all suggesting an engineer's precise and disciplined approach.

The book recommends basswood, a species used by Scheeler for many years. There is also mention, probably for the first time, of a wood called jelutong, a Malaysian species that Scheeler did not enjoy working. Burk never mentioned a wood called tupelo gum, which Louisiana carvers harvest from the swamps. The last fifteen carvings or so of Scheeler's were made from this wood.

Many of the techniques described in *Game Bird Carving* are in use today. The book describes knifework, shaping bodies with rasps, even using tracing-paper layouts for feather patterns, though Scheeler was to substitute Mylar, a transparent polyester sheet, for tracing paper and use the Foredom in place of the rasp.

Burk describes burning as time-consuming and tedious but effective for textural details. He recommends a small Unger soldering iron, the kind used by Jack Drake; Scheeler replaced it with more sophisticated burning tools. Burk puts the emphasis, however, on what he calls "gouge carving." Pictured in this book are Iski's old-squaw pair, unpainted.

Wendell Gilley wrote what is considered to be the first how-to book on bird carving. *The Art of Bird Carving: A Guide to a Fascinating Hobby* predates Burk's book by eleven years. The book was revised and reissued in 1972.

Gilley was a native of Southwest Harbor, Maine. Born in 1904, he hunted birds, did taxidermy work, owned a plumbing company and, by the time he died in 1983, had carved over 6,000 birds. They included life-size eagles, songbirds, gamebirds, and shorebirds. Scheeler knew Gilley and enjoyed his carvings.

In his revised book Gilley wrote that he had purchased a Foredom, the handpiece of which he showed in a photo. Even then it had the foot rheostat and the 14,000-rpm motor. The cutters, he added, came from Sears, Roebuck. But, like Burk, Gilley limited the use of the machine. For him it was best used making holes for glass eyes, drilling holes for leg wires, making the slots for open wings, and shaping and sanding places hard to reach with a knife or gouge.

On page 60 of the book there is a photograph of a Canada goose's wing. The barb and quill lines were clearly done with a burning tool. In the text Gilley wrote that a friend from Arizona had sent him a burning pen. When Gilley first saw burning, he said, he thought the lines had been made with a very fine **V** tool. The friend from Arizona might well have been Jack Drake. But Gilley, like Burk, considered burning time consuming and recommended it only for large birds, apparently because the Unger burning tool scores lines in wood that are too big for miniature birds or small songbirds.

One other major book came out in the 1970s. Called *Wildlife in Wood,* by Richard LeMaster from Illinois, this 1978 text might better have been titled "A Wildfowl Anatomy Lesson." There are hundreds of photos of duck profiles, rear- and top-view shots of waterfowl, and close-ups. The book offers shots of sleeping, aggressive, even frightened poses.

LeMaster was a master photographer and had learned to get a duck to pose in a glass-enclosed tank. He included close-ups of feather patterns, feather groupings, and leg textures.

In a how-to section, secondary to the bird photos, LeMaster showed a band saw in use as well as a flexible shaft handpiece removing sharp corners and shaping the head and bill of a duck. He also introduced a multiline burner, one with a series of scoring elements on the tip. But the burner never came into vogue with carvers, who found the lines it made too stiff looking.

What is interesting is that LeMaster encouraged the use of inserted primaries and tertials, something that Burk did not encourage and was not even mentioned by Gilley.

Taking Issue with Inserts

There is no doubt that Maggioni revolutionized the look of birds with his insertion techniques. And, of course, Scheeler became a master of inserts, achieving a high point of realism in his flying grouse and his goshawk and crow compositions.

But inserts have not been the only answer for carvers, including Scheeler. The best way to understand the complexity of feather insertion is to start with the bird itself. All birds' wings have a regular arrangement and specific number of feathers. Songbirds, known in scientific circles as passerines, have ten primaries, though in some families the tenth, or outermost, is greatly reduced in size. The number of secondaries varies more than the number of primaries: Hummingbirds have as few as six and some albatrosses have as many as forty. Most songbirds have nine.

Scheeler was influenced by Barth's method of carving the wings of his flying birds without inserts. Barth did this flying screech owl with moth in 1984. In the collection of Andy and Sandy Andrews.

As Maggioni described to Scheeler, on the top side of a wing, marginal coverts, lesser coverts, median coverts and greater coverts overlap from top to bottom. In addition, there are tertial and scapular feathers. The underside, or lining, includes similar sets of coverts and a group called axillars.

A cross section of a wing reveals that feathers within those layers can add up to nearly 100. Reproducing them would seem an impossible task, but that is what Maggioni in fact accomplished.

Though he and Scheeler inserted row upon row of feathers, including most of the coverts, carvers started carving the coverts into the solid wing structure. The procedure obviously consumes less time. But a more valid reason has been that coverts are fluffy and lacy in appearance, characteristics lost when the feathers are made into inserts.

One of Scheeler's most successful flying birds is this chukar partridge done in 1985. Feathers were carved as groups and inserted. In the collection of Andy and Sandy Andrews.

Maggioni, limited by the tools and wood he used, thought that inserts could best reproduce the complexity of feathers separating from the wing structure. With the high-speed bits, saws, cutters, and burrs marketed today as well as the availability of tupelo gum, a Southern wood that holds detail the way no other wood can, carvers can achieve precision impossible only a decade ago. Fine bits and small-diameter saws can transform a solid block of wood, even a species that is not tupelo, into highly detailed feather groupings.

Greater Realism

In addition to the new materials and tools, other trends in the bird carving world have suggested what to insert and how to do it. One dominant approach has avoided individually inserted pieces to achieve greater realism. Separate feather groupings within a large wing or tail are carved from a single piece of wood and then attached or inserted. Scheeler used this method with a broad-winged hawk in 1986. Each wing was carved from a solid piece of tupelo gum and attached to the body. The tail feathers were also carved from a solid block of wood and attached.

But the broad-wing was not posed as a flying bird. It was set on a base with its wings near the body. If the bird had been flying, could Scheeler have made realistic wings without inserts?

As people like Scheeler were striving for greater realism, they began to take a closer look at the birds they were copying, including the anatomy of a bird's flight feathers. At rest, these feathers do not lie adjacent to each other. Rather, they overlap and underlap to improve flight efficiency. On the downstroke feathers close tight, increasing

Below left *The top side of the wing shows that the feathers were not made as separate pieces.* Below *A detail of the feather groups.*

air friction, and on the upstroke they separate, much like fingers on a hand, to decrease air resistance. To allow for this complicated alignment, the individual feathers are shaped in cross section like an **S**.

Working with inserts to recreate flight feathers, as Scheeler discovered, can have its advantages. The **S** curve, with its convex shape on one side of the shaft and a concave shape on the other, can be carved from a reasonably thick insert. The longitudinal bend that comes with wing flapping can be accomplished by lightly wetting, bending and hot-air drying a thin insert so it will hold that shape. This was a technique developed by Scheeler.

Unfortunately, wood, even tupelo gum, lacks all the structural properties of feathers. A feather carved with an **S** curve cannot be steam-bent along the shaft. The wood cannot accommodate this compound curve.

Not unlike the goshawk and crow in composition, the sharp-shinned hawk and dead starling were done by Scheeler in 1985. In the collection of Andy and Sandy Andrews.

Thicker feather groupings, made in solid arrangements that can be inserted, have been the answer to this problem. A thick piece of wood gives enough body so that both the **S** curve and the bend along the shaft can be recreated for feathers in a group. Not surprisingly, the results have been a more sculpted look.

Though Drake made wings out of one piece of wood, even for flying birds, and Burk did the same with his wing-spreading, standing birds, it was Larry Barth who did such an anatomically convincing job with a flying screech owl in 1983 that Scheeler started moving away from inserts. When Scheeler made a flying chukar partridge in 1985, he used one piece of wood for the three end primaries, one piece for the seven other primaries, and one piece for the secondaries. It is considered among his best and most convincing flying wildfowl.

Scheeler liked what he called the sculpted look of the partridge. In an interview he said: "Without inserts there are fewer seams to hide. It's hard to get the transition from carved to inserted feathers. Without inserts you keep the bird more consistent looking." Even more to the point, he added: "Why insert when you don't have to?"

Yet Scheeler came up with a unique compromise when doing what he became best remembered for, his perching raptors. He carved the bird and its primaries as one piece, then cut away the two primary groups. He finished the primaries from two separate pieces of wood and then attached them to the body. This extra work allowed him to add details under the primaries impossible to reach with the wing still attached to the body. By carving the primaries on the bird in the first place, he saw exactly how the feathers flowed into the body.

But there are special effects to contend with in bird carving.

It was necessary for Scheeler to insert the body feathers on the starling.

Plumes on wading birds, for instance, most certainly require inserts, usually the use of a material other than wood, such as metal. Ruffled body feathers are another special effect. In 1986 Scheeler made a sharp-shinned hawk, wings spread, over a dead starling, the first return to his predator–prey composition since the goshawk and crow done in 1981. And like the crow of the earlier piece, the starling has feathers spread apart, indicating a "ruined" look. Scheeler inserted all but the starling's head feathers. He made the inserts out of slivers of triangular tupelo and overlapped them like shingles. The thin, crisp body feathers, disarrayed in death, are an effect not easily achieved from a solid block of wood.

The New Generation

Scheeler was a innovator, an experimenter, and also a supporter. He kept in touch with a great number of carvers regularly. He did so not through the mail, for Scheeler was not fond of writing. Instead, his telephone became a switchboard through which bird carvers could share ideas and techniques. And it did not bother Scheeler that his phone bill went as high as $500 a month.

One of the carvers Scheeler talked to frequently was Larry Barth. Winner of the 1985 and 1986 World titles, Barth first saw Scheeler's work—the prairie falcon over a mourning dove—when he was a teenager. Much like Drake, Barth had been carving in isolation, so he was in awe of what people like Scheeler were creating. When he went to college, he helped design a program for himself that included sculpture, design, color, and avian anatomy. His undergraduate senior art project was a great horned owl family, an adult and two baby owls. The story behind them has become a paradigm of ingenuity and something that won the respect of Scheeler.

Barth wanted to give the baby birds a fluffy appearance, something no other carver had succeeded in doing. Perhaps he had seen a Popsicle stick chewed and frayed on its end. He imagined that balsa fibers would separate as easily. Manually fraying small pieces of the wood met with little success. He then chewed them with better results. But each "tuft" of wood took about ten minutes, and at the rate he was going, he anticipated it would take six months to finish enough wood for the two birds. More experimentation showed that boiling the balsa strips before chewing cut the time needed to fray the ends to ten seconds, although it took five hours of boiling the strips to get them ready for chewing.

Barth put the family of owls in the 1979 World Championship Wildfowl Carving Competition, the first contest he ever entered. The piece came in second behind Forehand's jungle fowl, but it caught the attention of the carving world, including Scheeler's. They stayed in close touch after that.

It was Barth who encouraged Scheeler to do more exacting study models in clay. Scheeler started doing so in 1986 with a pair of mourning doves that never found their way into wood. But the man whom Barth was to call a Zen master proved, as he had in the past, that he was willing to try the techniques of others.

Another carver Scheeler talked with frequently was Robert Guge. From Illinois, Guge was a musician and an industrial painter, as Scheeler had been before he started carving full time. Guge's first competition bird was a canvasback duck. The pattern for it was traced from Burk's *Game Bird Carving*. Guge went on to become a World champion.

In 1979 the World Show created a miniatures category in addition to the decorative life-size division. The miniatures category was given a World-Class table, and Guge took the miniatures title three times: first in 1984 with a pair of mourning doves, second in 1986 with three puffins (Scheeler was one of the three judges for miniatures that year), and last in 1987, when Guge entered a pair of bluebirds.

Scheeler had not made any ducks since the early 1970s with the exception of a black duck he worked on during the last few years of his life. But Scheeler was especially impressed with the ducks of William Schultz's son Marc. Scheeler went so far as to call them "jewels," among the best carved waterfowl he had ever seen.

Marc Schultz, who lives in Wisconsin, won the World title for decorative floating waterfowl in 1986 with a pair of cinnamon teals. The following year he came in second with a pair of scaup.

Schultz specializes in the art of burning. He discovered that bringing together the components of fine burning and oil paints could replicate or at least suggest soft feathers that few other carvers had achieved. To do this requires him to burn lines so close together that in some areas there are no fewer than 220 lines per inch. Scheeler, by comparison, burned up to 80 lines for the same space.

Though Scheeler felt he could never do such fine burning, he did ask Schultz to share his formulas for mixing oil paints. The results were to Scheeler's liking.

When Barton Walter of Virginia finished his two life-size Canada geese in 1986, Scheeler said they were among the finest decorative bird carvings he had seen. The geese, which took eleven months to complete, were started as clay models. The raised wing of one bird was made from a single piece of wood inserted into the body block. The primaries and tertials are all out of one piece, and some of the tail feathers were carved separately. The painting took roughly 200 hours. Some of Walter's painting strategy came from Scheeler.

Another outstanding Walter composition is a life-size great blue heron and female red-winged black bird. The shorebird's plumes are made from pieces of brass and inserted. Scheeler thought this, too, was an outstanding piece. It was entered in the 1983 World Championships but came in second to Rudisill's black-crowned night herons. Walter was only twenty-five years old that year.

Among the other carvers Scheeler called regularly were his friends from Louisiana, the Brunets. He admired the work of Tan Brunet and his son, Jett. The elder Brunet is a carver who probably did as much for waterfowl carvers as Scheeler did for carvers doing birds of prey.

Brunet, a Cajun, developed his own style of texturing in the early 1970s. While Burk and Drake and Scheeler were using an Unger soldering iron, Brunet was using ice picks heated on the kitchen stove. But he, like Schultz, saw how burning lines can interact with wood and paint to create a soft look for feathers. The results won him five World Championships for his floating waterfowl: the first in 1977 with a pair of pintails, the second in 1978 with a pair of mallards. In 1981 he came back with a pair of canvasbacks and won for the third time, followed by a winning pair of green-winged teals in 1982, and finally, in 1983, a pair of redheads.

Jett Brunet was to develop his own style of waterfowl carving, one that was no less convincing than his father's. In 1985 he entered the World Class with a pair of ruddy ducks and won the $10,000 purchase prize. He came in third in 1986, but he won the grand prize again in 1987 with his scaup pair.

The Brunets were not the only waterfowl carvers Scheeler kept in close touch with. Pat Godin was another World-Class winner

Scheeler was to have a strong impact on a Vermont carver named Floyd Scholz. Scholz, who talked frequently with Scheeler, did these egrets in 1986. In the collection of Dr. and Mrs. Myron Yanoff, Philadelphia, Pennsylvania.

whom Scheeler called frequently. In 1976 Godin won the World Class with a pair of goldeneyes, in 1980 with a pair of black ducks. But these birds were a departure from previous ones. They interacted. The hen of the species has a dragonfly nymph in her bill, and the drake swims after her.

In 1982 Godin returned to The World with another pair of black ducks. These were standing, confronting a muskrat. The composition was put in the decorative life-size category and won.

Two of the last people Scheeler spoke to before his death were Maryland carver Habbart Dean, vice-chairman of the Ward Foundation, and Floyd Scholz of Vermont. Scheeler shared with Dean a number of techniques, including feather insertions. With Scholz the discussions centered on raptors, which are Scholz's favorite birds. Scholz first saw Scheeler's work in a Connecticut Audubon exhibit in 1975, when he was only seventeen years old. Interestingly, the piece he most remembers was the same piece Barth had seen at almost the same time but in a different state. It is the prairie falcon and mourning dove. Scholz was to use the predator–prey formula for two major carvings, one of them a gyrfalcon and dead puffin, which he started almost immediately after Scheeler died and finished in time for entry in the World Show of 1987.

Scholz also brought to that World Show a pair of egrets. Though this composition was very different from the Louisiana herons Scheeler had carved in 1983, the influence was evident. Scheeler's design and composition techniques, which had dominated the bird carving world for fifteen years, were being accepted and modified by a new generation of carvers.

The Last Frontier

Barth has made a profound impact on bird carving, particularly with philosophy. He has said that for him techniques are "on the back burner. They will continue to simmer there. But when you get to a certain level, the last frontier is composition."

Barth believes that making the jump from bird carving to sculpture is a mental leap more than a technical one. He explains by examining his own evolution as an artist. His original interest in birds was their colors. That interest translated into two-dimensional work, which in turn moved him to three-dimensional art, which refocused his interest on shape and form, not necessarily colors. Two of his major pieces, the snowy owl and bonaparte's gull, and his two common terns, are clean lined, white and patternless. They are not heavily vermiculated birds, like the woodcocks he used to do, birds with complex plumage. The pedestal for the terns he calls a classic sculptural presentation.

Barth also sees a minimalist approach with that kind of base. It is devoid of stones, ground material, vegetation, resinous water, branches, and insects, all elements of many major pieces made during the last decade and a half of bird carving. Though Barth has articulated so well this concept of composition, Scheeler was not only aware of it but also put it into practice early on with his decorative pieces.

An Abstract Flash

American painter Andrew Wyeth has used the expression "abstract flash" to describe an elusive something caught by the corner of the eye, a fleeting glimpse of something seldom if ever seen. Translating the elusive into the concrete would describe what Scheeler was doing with his predators and prey. He brought them into full focus by posing the birds so that they would become not elusive but lucid. To do this successfully, he had to put form and shape above all other considerations. Though the plumage should be textured and rendered in paints fairly accurately, the birds had to have strong poses.

Douglas Miller had Scheeler's prairie falcon cast in bronze. That the falcon was looking up was no accident. It tells the story of interruption and distraction. No paint or texture is needed to tell the story. The same is true of the dove, with its wings curving upward. The cactus plants add interest, but are by no means necessary.

Scheeler did not create this falcon by suggestion. The prairie falcon is unquestionably a prairie falcon. But it was probably the earliest piece in which he became less tied to physical fact than to form.

Another outstanding piece is an Arctic gyrfalcon on a rock. Made in 1980, it is a moment in the bird's life, its only habitat being that stone. Scheeler was careful to balance the masses of hard and soft form, making it another excellent example of his understanding of sculpture.

Scheeler did not stop with the gyrfalcon when experimenting with balancing masses. He was most conscious of this concept when doing his pair of surf scoters. Scheeler balanced not only soft and hard masses—each bird sits on a rock—but also color. Scoters are almost crow-black, whereas the rocks he painted were white and gray. The birds are like bronzes, shapes without color. Yet their forms tell a simple story of alertness, suggesting possible intrusion into their sea world.

Color Theory

Scheeler was not opposed to making colorful birds. Many of the ducks he chose were colorful, including a pair of wood ducks, considered gaudy by many artists. But one of his most successful birds is a blue heron. His painting style made strong use of oil paints, resulting in colors and patterns that appeared bolder than they really were. This made the bird project from the composition. His very last bird was a peregrine falcon, hardly a drab bird.

Nor was the green heron he did in 1983 a monochromatic bird. For this one he chose habitat that would complement the bird, or rather the bird complemented the flowers, since he made them first. He chose pitcher plants that have colors similar to the heron's.

But Scheeler most enjoyed putting into opposition the elements of light and dark. It is hardly coincidental that his 1974 Arctic gyrfalcon and oldsquaw show such contrasts. The falcon is predominantly white with dark feather patterns. The oldsquaw has large areas of dark and white plumage.

For his 1981 goshawk composition, he chose a crow to enhance the light coloration of the hawk rather than a vermiculated bird, such as a quail or grouse. Yet the black represents a powerful statement of death. It is difficult to say that the goshawk is the dominant feature of the carving. Through good design, Scheeler once again created a careful balance of light and dark forms.

Fugue in Flight

Flight has its own artistic theories. McKoy's covey of thirteen bobwhite quail is not just a representation of a hunter's intrusion. Nor is it just an engineered sculpture or a fleeting moment in the birds' natural history. The composition suggests a fugue: that is, a repetition of themes as the flight of the quail is successively developed upward.

At first it would seem that a single theme, a quail rise, is exploited. The individual quail burst from the ground in close succession, but as the birds rise, a greater degree of freedom is achieved. Like a fugue, then, a term that derives from the Latin word *fugere,* meaning "to fly," there is a series of initially compressed flights, each flight offering a differing or contrasting element to the preceding episodes. Thus continuity from one bird to another is maintained. The uppermost bird is some four feet above the base, seemingly free, yet it cannot be seen out of its context. It is a restatement of all the lower birds of the covey rise.

Scheeler's two flying terns, in contrast, show a display of aggression. They are, like Forehand's jungle fowl and Rudisill's clapper rails, in conflict. But Scheeler did not pursue this theme. Likely, he saw the terns as visually complex images. And perhaps there was too much going on.

Above left *Scheeler explored the theme of flight with a number of compositions. This is a pair of green-winged teals he did in the 1970s. In the collection of the Wildlife World Museum.* Above *A rear view of the lower bird. Its suspension wire is concealed in the "water," or epoxy resin.* Left *The lower bird and the splash made from the epoxy resin.*

An earlier Scheeler piece has two green-winged teals taking off. Both describe the act, but there is an imbalance. The lower teal still has contact with the water, whereas the other is very high up. The distance between the waterfowl is discomforting.

When he returned to doing a pair of flying birds, he offered a twofold theme of flight with his ruffed grouse. Rather than developing the birds only upward, he has them flying away from each other. Yet they are far from mirror images, for each describes, through its wing positions, a different story of flight. There is a balance of action in a limited space. But unlike McKoy's quail, the time interval is the same.

Another view of the upper bird.

Life and Death in Avian Art

Though death in art is disquieting on the whole, it is a fact of natural history. Early pieces by Maggioni and McKoy depict struggles between birds or between birds and other animals. For the most part these are large pieces set in museumlike dioramas of undefined boundaries. It was in 1977, when Rudisill exhibited his pair of clapper rails, that the struggle was confined to a base instead of a case and the habitat became not a field but a simple suggestion of marsh.

Still, the trend was away from battles and toward the moments after death. Scheeler depicted life and death for the first time in 1973 with his peregrine and green-winged teals and the last time in 1986 with the sharp-shinned hawk and starling. Gary Yoder of Maryland was successful with the predator–prey theme on a miniature scale. In 1985 he brought to the World Competition a diminutive Cooper's hawk and flicker. One foot of the hawk is planted on the breast of the songbird. It took Best in World Miniature that year.

Left *The bird is suspended with the aid of a steel tail feather and a metal stem.* Below *The inserted wing.*

Above *Scheeler was one of the first bird carvers to explore the theme of life and death. This is an early goshawk and blue-winged teal. In the collection of the Wildlife World Museum.* Above right *Scheeler's sharp-shinned hawk and evening grosbeak is typical of his predator–prey theme.*

Guge used the idea of raptor and prey with two major pieces. One shows a kestrel with a goldfinch tucked underneath it. The other shows a mantling kestrel with a grasshopper in its talons.

The Power of Simplicity

These predator–prey carvings are fairly devoid of habitat. Such is the case with almost all of Scheeler's predator–prey compositions, with the exception of the cactus in the prairie falcon and dove piece. What Scheeler understood early on was that a simple composition is a powerful means of expression. He wanted no landscapes with these birds. What he did achieve was a way of translating the intensity of the kill into wood. And that is one of the reasons he was so comfortable with raptors. His skills enabled him to capture wild, fierce, intelligent, defiant looks in the faces of his hawks and falcons. This ability is probably one of the reasons he considered his Harris' hawk his most successful work. The eyes glare, the beak is open. At its feet is a dead rabbit, which, incidentally, is a light form in contrast to the dark shape of the raptor.

Above left *Gary Yoder of Maryland, who was strongly influenced by Scheeler, did this miniature composition of Cooper's hawk and flicker for the World Championship of 1985. It won Best in World, Miniature Wildfowl. In the collection of the North American Wildfowl Art Museum. Above William Schultz also used the predator–prey theme with this black-shouldered kite and frog. In the collection of the Wildlife World Museum. Left Floyd Scholz did this kestrel and dragonfly in 1986. In the collection of Richard and Dorothy Robson, Hancock, Vermont.*

In the Round

Below *In the 1970s the carving world adopted the notion that bird compositions could be observed from any angle. One of the trend setters in this area was Lynn Forehand. A stunning example of birds in flight and observable from any angle are his three mourning doves. In the collection of the Wildlife World Museum.* Below right *Scheeler was not too concerned with the in-the-round design. But the trend continued. Forehand also did these battling grebes. Note that one duck is under the water. In the collection of the Wildlife World Museum.*

Despite his concentration on form, nearly all of Scheeler's pieces have a definite front and back: that is, for the full meaning of the compositions to be imparted, they are best observed from a limited point of view. What is unusual about Forehand's jungle fowl, and his two compositions of three mourning doves and three Ross' gulls in flight, is that the birds can be observed from different angles without losing the message or theme.

Bird artists like Forehand have frequently designed compositions so that they could be viewed from a number of perspectives while their moment in time or natural history is not lost to a back or an unpleasing side. This is more readily achieved with two similar birds rather than one. A single "live" bird must ultimately have its back to the viewer.

The front–back perspective didn't particularly bother Scheeler when it came to doing hawks. Inspired by large, staring eyes, he wanted them to be looked at, confronted if you will. The real workmanship was done in their faces.

But had Scheeler designed in-the-round pieces, he would have needed a turntable or mirror or both to allow him to view his work

quickly in the round. McKoy used a turntable for his quail covey. Guge has also favored in-the-round designs and has used them for two or three birds. His Best-in-World pair of mourning doves, for instance, are at a mountain runoff, complete with rocks and resinous water. Another piece shows three burrowing owls interacting. Entitled "Two for Approval," the piece has two immature owls bringing home food to the mother. Were lines drawn from all three pairs of eyes, the lines would intersect in the center of the composition. And for a third in-the-round piece, his 1986 Best in World, Guge made use of three common puffins.

Spirals, S Curves, and Circles

When Guge's puffins are examined more closely, the viewer immediately notices that these three seabirds are at different heights. The black-and-white birds on sea-gray rock bring the eye up and around as if following a spiral. Necks and bodies are turned or positioned so that they, too, contribute to the spiraling composition.

Geometric shapes play no small role in bird art. In 1980 Gary Yoder put two miniature pheasants in flight, one above the other. Rather than making a linear departure, as is the case with many of McKoy's quail, Yoder's birds effect a strong vertical spiral. What contributes to the design are the pheasants' long tail feathers, which twist and turn as the birds soar sharply upward above a cornstalk.

A bird might suggest yet another geometrical shape: the S curve. The pair of mourning doves Scheeler put on a twisty branch has tails and heads turning in opposite directions, suggesting the reverse curve of an S. Yet Scheeler moderated the action by bringing the wings of

Above left Guge also did a circular arrangement of three burrowing owls. Lines drawn from the three pairs of eyes would meet in the center of the composition. In the collection of Andy and Sandy Andrews. Above *The necks of these miniature least bitterns by Muehlmatt suggest S curves. They won Best in World, Miniature Wildfowl, 1981. In the collection of the North American Wildfowl Art Museum.*

*Muehlmatt's circular arrangement
of five bobwhite quail suggests the
discovery of an intruder. These
took Best in World, Decorative
Lifesize, 1984. In the collection of
the North American Wildfowl
Art Museum.*

both birds out slightly, which helps bracket the composition and
keeps the eye from getting confused.

A composition that used necks to fulfill the **S** curve was made in
1981 by Ernest Muehlmatt. Least bitterns assume an upright freeze
posture at the approach of danger. This posture works with their
long necks, coloring, and habitat of tall grasses to create a natural
camouflage. Muehlmatt's birds have **S**-curving necks that are symmetrical to one another.

Long flexing necks offer a strong design component in Scheeler's
Louisiana herons. Though the birds neither fly nor interact, they do
display a pleasing symmetry. Their off-center, **S**-curving necks suggest spirals. But they also carry the eye from the body mass through
the heads and directional bills down to the long legs and feet, where
the eye can again move up the body. Consequently, Scheeler achieved
a circularity; the eye need not move off the composition.

This spiraling composition has Yoder's two miniature pheasants taking off from a cornfield. They won Best in World, Miniature Wildfowl, 1980. In the collection of the North American Wildfowl Art Museum.

There is an implied circularity with Scheeler's goshawk and crow. The dead bird's wings sweep upward as it lies on its back. But the goshawk is mantling, a protective posture in which the wings spread partially out and down. The birds' wings, then, complement each other and give unity to these very different species, one alive, the other dead.

Muehlmatt made use of circular design in his 1984 Best-in-World composition, titled "Needles, Feathers, and Bone." Instead of having the five bobwhite quail interact with one another or putting them in flight, he has them at a particular moment of discovery: An unseen intruder has come upon them. The quail are, in various stages, aware of the interloper.

This awareness might be described as the inner story or message, but an outer story or physical theme is also apparent. The quail are in a desert setting. A leafless desert wood called manzanita twists its way skyward behind a cow's skull. Cactus segments make the piece reminiscent of Scheeler's prairie falcon and dove, but the comparison ends there. Muehlmatt was looking for a strong statement of habitat as well as a color complement to the browns and umbers of the birds. Throughout the composition there is a tension between life and desolation, which will be resolved if the birds decide to break out into flight, as McKoy's quail did.

For the moment, however, a hen has her head turned around in a resting position. Trying to keep from sliding off a sandy slope, she stretches one leg out to keep her balance. Immediately to her left, an alert bird peers over the cow's skull. Yet another quail is on top of the skull, looking directly at the intruder, and at the viewer. And two other quail to the right are also aware of a presence.

Not by accident are these birds at different heights and placed around and on top of the skull. When the eye explores the composition, it is unconsciously led around and back again. A circularity is achieved and the eye is kept on the piece.

It has been written that much of art comprises tension and resolution, a theme that Scheeler used with many of his major carvings. That theme also applies to another composition of five birds. Floyd Scholz has used puffins to tell a story of discovery in a 1986 composition. Like Guge's seabirds, Scholz's are on high rocks. But unlike Muehlmatt's quail composition, Scholz's includes the interloper, a crab, which is quite visible and a definitive part of the story.

As the crab crosses a rock face below the birds, the puffin closest to the crab and lowest in the composition is balanced on one foot, ready to jump up and away. Another bird, higher up, is curious without the tenseness of the previous puffin and has determined that there is no threat. The bird has resolved the issue by not retreating. The other three puffins, out of what Scholz calls "a zone of action," bring the eye to the top of the rocks not in a straight line but in a spiral.

More on Flying Birds

With a mallard composition done in 1982, Yoder was successful in dealing with birds that neither spiral nor are victor and vanquished. In what he describes as a free-form piece, one that does not have a geometric design, two mallards are about to land on a pond. Part of a unidirectional composition, these birds do not touch, as his pheasants do. Nor are they as compactly designed as his spiraling pheasants. However, their wings are designed to portray the two basic positions for flight: the upstroke, which opens the feathers to reduce wind resistance, and the downstroke, which closes the feathers for aerodynamic thrust. It is as if a viewer were watching a comple-

Much as Scheeler did, Gary Yoder explored the dynamics of flight. His two mallards are what he calls a free-form composition. The birds took Best in World, Miniature Wildfowl, in 1982. In the collection of the North American Wildfowl Art Museum.

mentary process in which each bird is describing half the action of flying.

But directional cues are not so easily overcome with a single flying bird. Beaks or bills point away from the bird, as do wing tips and tails. Scheeler would seem to have solved this problem with a flying willet he did in 1983. Supported by a twisty piece of marsh grass, the bird is neither escaping from the earth nor landing, both of which would strongly suggest direction. Rather, it is gliding, its wings gently arcing downward. Those wing curves, the curves of the grass stems, even the spiraling curve of a piece of weathered wood below the shorebird all keep the viewer focused on the main element of the composition. Also minimized is what some critics describe as that uneasy feeling of flight, which is the building up and releasing of tension through the action of flight feathers.

With twisty wood and curving grass and wings, Scheeler's willet is an excellent example of how to deal with flight. The point of contact between wings and grass is minimal. In the collection of the North American Wildfowl Art Museum.

The Essence of a Bird

Yoder was not the only artist to portray an essential behavioral mechanism using two birds. Scheeler did this with his ruffed grouse, as have other carvers with other birds. William Schultz showed the process of preening in a 1982 composition of two red-breasted geese. Preening, for waterfowl, means cleaning the feathers and rubbing them with an oil produced by a gland at the base of the tail. One bird, however, cannot convey the two-stage process. Schultz carved the two birds so that the position of each bird complements the other. Preening is described in its entirety.

Another early Scheeler flying bird is this mourning dove. In the collection of the Wildlife World Museum.

By the 1980s the message was clear to bird carvers. The emphasis would be on capturing the essence of a bird, either in an animated or a quiet pose, perhaps at a moment in its natural history but without the violent conflict and complicated habitat displays.

Still, artists today struggle with the single bird, claiming that it is not easy to bring across the essence and character of a solitary animal. To understand how carvers have dealt with the problem, Scheeler included, consider how they have worked with a particular species, first in pairs of birds and finally one bird at a time.

In 1976 McKoy first exhibited a composition of two clapper rails fighting for possession of a crab. On a round walnut base filled with simulated mud, the birds' bodies and wings seem entwined in conflict while the crab forms a bridge between their outstretched bills.

Two years later Rudisill created his two clapper rails in conflict over a snail. Their base contains marsh grasses and oyster shells. Compositionally, there is balance and display as the two birds, facing each other with wings spread, vie for food. And in keeping with Rudisill's design theories, the piece is designed to be viewed in the round.

In 1983 Scheeler composed a single clapper rail. Often heard at night in salt marshes, this bird makes a harsh, chattering sound.

Left *As Scheeler explored flight with two birds of the same species, William Schultz examined preening behavior with these two red-breasted geese. In the collection of the Wildlife World Museum. Above Scheeler never stopped trying to capture the essence of wildfowl. Having observed that the clapper rail is a noisy bird, he made its beak open and its expression antagonistic. This 1983 carving is ready to take off. In the collection of the North American Wildfowl Art Museum.*

Scheeler's rail, wings outspread, utters a soundless cry as it steps forward on one foot in preparation for flight.

The character of his clapper rail is easily established. But while designing the composition, Scheeler edited out anything that might act as a distraction on the base, giving only a hint of habitat by using moss and a pair of oyster shells. The terrain is sparse and the action is strongly above the base. Scheeler evokes the setting of the marsh, though it is almost inconspicuous; the eye remains entertained by the action of the rail. The base is abstract, adding only secondary interest to the overall piece.

Many of Scheeler's single birds are studies in motion. With this roadrunner, Scheeler created the illusion of pursuit. In the collection of the Wildlife World Museum.

Confined Animation

Scheeler continued to work with what he called confined animation. For him this technique reached a peak with his long-eared owl and mouse composition. Well balanced, the owl appears nearly weightless as it begins its flight. The same feeling is captured with the clapper rail. Scheeler also worked on a design similar to the owl's with a sharp-shinned hawk, though the composition never got beyond a clay body and metal wings.

A Scheeler composition that dates back to the late 1970s is a roadrunner. Not unlike the later clapper rail, the bird is moving forward in pursuit of a lizard. Yet the prey is unnecessary. The implied sense of motion in the roadrunner is a statement in itself.

Scheeler was to state, after he had finished the clapper rail, that life is motion, and birds in particular do not stand still. Both roadrunner and rail are on one foot, wings away from the body. But the rail has its beak open, the tongue extended. It is a much more animated pose.

More than a Bird on a Base

Despite their best efforts at design and composition, carvers make many pieces that are no more than a painted and detailed bird on a branch on a wooden base. Scheeler did a kestrel in 1983 that fits that formula. From a round base rises a weathered branch. At its top, perched on one foot, is the kestrel.

That bird art has been stereotyped into a bird on a stick on a base may first have been put into words by Barth. But carvers have suspected for some time that something was amiss with the bird–stick–

base formula after hearing more praise for the piece of driftwood than for the bird itself. Scheeler himself claimed to have heard such praise for one of his compositions. Or undue praise is offered for the base, which has its own mundane formula: a round, elliptical, or octagonal, often segmented piece of walnut or mahogany.

A goshawk Scheeler worked on in 1986 perches on a branch. But the bough is not visible. Nor does the branch rise up out of the base. Instead, it appears out of the background, descends, and touches a corner of the base's top. Scheeler, who called this composition a vignette, explained that the wood bypasses the base to create the illusion of a branch that hangs down. Whether the branch and bird are twenty, forty, or a hundred feet off the ground is subject to the imagination of the viewer. It is a powerful illusion and a logical way of dealing with the immensities of nature.

Interestingly, the branch that Scheeler made was not a found item but one he designed and carved to effect the right look and

A different approach to a roadrunner: It's not in pursuit. This one was carved by Scheeler's friend William Koelpin of Wisconsin.

shape. The base also defies the bird-on-a-stick-on-a-base formula, for it is neither round nor elliptical. Instead, it is an oblong block of teakwood, suggesting a platform for sculpture. His mourning dove pair is mounted on a squarish block of blackened wood, as is his last composition, a peregrine falcon. Despite the implications of what Barth and others have heard from critics, the sticks are getting fancier and the bases more artistic.

Above *Guge gave height to a miniature cardinal with a simple limb and black base, done in 1986.* Above right *Barth carved water on the surface of his walnut base in this 1983 composition of a kingfisher.* Right *Eldridge Arnold was a forerunner in simplifying bases and making them look sculptural. In 1983 he put this woodcock on a black marble base.*

More Artistic Uses of Habitat

Both Scheeler and Barth incorporated pine needles into their compositions, Barth with a flying screech owl and Scheeler with a merlin. They not only suggest the natural history of the bird but also complement the denser birds. In addition, the green of the needles complements many bird colors.

Barth went to the 1987 World Championships with a pair of blackburnian warblers mounted on what Barth describes as "an abstract flourish." A hemlock branch, made of brass with copper wire needles and tupelo cones, cascades from space and lightly touches an oblong black base. The brightly colored birds perch on the hemlock. Yet the coniferous branch in no way overwhelms the warblers. The entire piece is a vignette that is both light and airy.

A piece that has been described as a bonsai arrangement was brought to the same show by Muehlmatt. His birds, stellar jays, are clumped on a square wooden base that in turn is set on a diminutive bonsai table. Though there is a branch that descends, touching one corner of the block, it is not hemlock but lodgepole pine. It was Scheeler who told him how to make the needles out of bamboo.

Above left *To give the illusion of height for this unfinished goshawk, Scheeler made a carved branch that came down and touched a simple black base.* Above *Barth wanted to give the illusion of height with a northern oriole in a cherry tree, done in 1983.*

Before using the sculptural base, carvers used turned or segmented bases and built their habitat on them. Koelpin wanted his mourning doves to look as though they were high in a tree, without using a tall branch.

The piece suggests a philosophy of arrangement that has shaped Muehlmatt's bird designs for more than a decade. It is Ikebana, the Japanese way of arranging flowers. Essential to the design are three focal points. One is the centerline, which is slightly to the right. This is described as heaven in the literature. Lower down is another mass called man and below that is a mass called earth. These three elements are the essence of the piece that Muehlmatt titled "The Middle Child."

Neither of these compositions won the World Championship: A pair of blue jays did. Created by a Canadian named Gordon Hare, the presentation at first seems simple. One jay, noisy and aggressive, is in a threatening, horizontal posture. The other, higher bird looks anticipatory.

Two birds on two sticks. A regression to the old formula? This is not the case, for not only are the two sticks unattached, but there is also a third branch, and none of them are on a base. They are self-supporting and movable. Hare's composition has become an abstract flash that the viewer can actually change. He has only to reach out and rearrange the branches. To use a photographic parallel, if the viewer were a camera, he could not only change the focal length but also the perspective.

Scheeler never saw Hare's "Hue and Cry: Blue Jay Pair." But he was always ready to praise new presentations. It is likely he would have been pleased.

Foliage can make strong suggestions, as it does in a 1985 kestrel composition by Guge. The green-painted cooper grasses on the base complement the colors of the bird above, but their wavy and bending design also leaves the viewer with the impression of a strong wind blowing in. Above the blades of grass is a kestrel, not at rest, like Scheeler's goshawk, but seeking balance on its branch.

In this composition there is a natural history, animation, a strongly designed bird with wings outstretched and arching to find balance, a branch that gives height without taking away from the kestrel, and a careful use of colors. All the components of bird, base, and branch work together.

Above left *Muehlmatt was influenced by Oriental flower arranging when he did these three stellar jays and lodgepole pine in 1987. In the collection of Andy and Sandy Andrews.* Above *With this 1985 merlin, Scheeler added pine needles to give an airy mass to the area below the bird. In the collection of Andy and Sandy Andrews.*

Above *Foliage contributes to this mantling kestrel done by Guge in 1985. The bent grasses suggest the wind that the hawk is trying to steady itself against. In the collection of Greg and Ellen Baron.* Right *Scheeler encouraged impressionistic bird carving. This 1987 redwood burl merganser was done by Leo and Lee Osborne of Maine.*

Beyond the Confines of a Base

Hare seemed almost defiant in removing his jays from the traditional base. Other artists have argued that bases too often restrict the bird and habitat to geometrically shaped pieces of wood. There have been notable exceptions other than Hare's. Two in particular are worthy of analysis. One sculpted base is, in fact, so much a part of the bird that the term "base" may not even apply.

The first is Barth's "Winter Lakeshore: Snowy Owl and Bonaparte's Gull." Instead of a hardwood geometric base, Barth put his owl and prey on a weathered piece of tree that sits not on finished wood but on sand.

Building up the height of the sand dune with a foundation of wood, Barth lets the sand trail off and feather out behind the bird of prey. What is achieved is perhaps more than a vignette. Barth has created a suggestion of expansiveness, contributed to by the weathered stump and wind-bent grasses. The components work well together, suggesting not only a lake shore setting but also starkness.

The second piece is by McKoy, made several years after he completed his covey of quail. A black skimmer, easily identifiable by its lower, fish-catching mandible knifing through the water, meets its base in mid-air. But the base mirrors the flying, painted skimmer. Though carved from walnut, it is a fluid image of the bird, supported on sculpted wings that flatten out in flight. The walnut bird is neither detailed nor painted, yet it is easily identified as a skimmer, and the lower mandibles of both birds are the only point of contact. Is the painted bird more important to the viewer? Or is the equally graceful and sculpted walnut image more exciting for what it suggests rather than defines anatomically? What if the piece were inverted and the walnut skimmer were to take to the air? Perhaps a new world would be created in which a surface lacking details reflected flight feathers and barb lines.

Au Naturel

McKoy was not the first to offer a wood carving that rendered only the impression of the bird. Birds done this way have origins from before the rise of agricultural societies. Yet today at bird exhibitions and contests, natural wood compositions may not receive the attention that the more decorated species get, though the carvings may be no less artistic. In fact, they are closer to a purely sculptural art form than even the most meticulously posed and detailed birds because there is no attempt to hide the materials used. It was Scheeler who encouraged this form of bird carving, and he was instrumental in getting the Ward Foundation to make a fourth World-Class division: Natural Finish Lifesize Wildfowl Sculpture.

For years Scheeler had admired the work of John Sharp. Once a full-time patternmaker, Sharp works with the form and essence of a bird rather than its plumage and coloring. His carvings are simple, often showing only the shape of a duck coming out of the top of a stump carved to simulate water. They are efficient, cleanly designed pieces, images of birds as an integral part of their environment.

Two other artist–carvers have been working in the 1980s to turn natural woods into bird forms. Leo and Lee Osborne, a husband-and-wife team, have shaped such unlikely wood pieces as burls to create the essence of a bird with grain, natural wood color, and even texture.

Using a redwood burl, the Osbornes portrayed a killdeer feigning a broken wing. The grain is erratic yet does not detract from the bird's distraction display. The Osbornes also made a merganser in extremely dense cherry burl.

In 1987 the Osbornes created a piece from a redwood burl. What they saw in the grain textures reminded them of the Maine coast: barnacles, mussels, rocks. The result was a composition called "Peep Show."

Scheeler's Last Bird

Scheeler probably would not have made natural wood carvings had he lived. However, he considered doing birds for bronzing, ones for which he would have economized on the use of textures and inserts.

Whatever he might have made, he would have put the essence of the bird foremost. This was the case with his last piece, a peregrine falcon. Obviously, he continued to have a passion for strong, powerful profiles and expressions of temperament. The peregrine is in an upright pose, perched on a rock balanced on a simple black base. It is a stark, linear piece, dramatic but restrained. The bird is muscular, strongly posed, its piercing eyes intent on something. It is a technically polished piece, for Scheeler did not economize on textures that

Above *The pose of this early peregrine falcon is not unlike the last bird Scheeler worked on, also a peregrine.* Above right *Scheeler seemed to be strengthening the pose of his raptors, as he did with this red-headed merlin made in the 1970s. In the collection of the Wildlife World Museum.*

move from coarse to very fine. The paint work is among the best he ever did, and the feathers are exquisitely rendered.

In this piece Scheeler continued to see sculpture as a network of contrasts. He used an almost exact balance of hard stone mass and soft bird mass. There are opposing light and dark values on the bird itself and between it and the rock. And the inanimate granite balances the depth of the peregrine's stare.

Artistically, Scheeler had come a long way from the peregrine he made in the early 1970s. Its simplistic pose and design remind the viewer of one of the Stone Age cave paintings of southern Europe. The handling of the subject matter is almost impressionistic. But it does not have the sculpted look of later hawks. An experiment in vertical design, the wood below the bird is too much like the peregrine in shape and texture. There is competition between bird and base.

To capture the intense stare of a bird of prey, Scheeler spent a great deal of time on the face.

A Simple Life

Scheeler was a family man. His wife, Edythe, supported his work, going to the exhibitions and contests with him and enjoying the recognition her husband received.

They met in 1947 in Mays Landing, New Jersey, while Scheeler was working on cars in a garage behind Edythe's parents' house. Edythe remembers his flat work, the duck boats he built, his hunting, his work in the flower gardens, his being a good father and husband.

During the last years, with most of their five children gone from the house, they had more time to share, though they relished the presence of grandchildren, whom Scheeler let into the shop as he worked.

In January 1987 Scheeler entered the hospital for surgery. The peregrine remained unfinished in his newly renovated shop. A pair of doves and a flying sharp-shinned hawk never evolved from clay. He died on the twenty-third of January.

PART TWO

Remembrances

Kenneth Scheeler

Julius Iski

Byron Cheever *for* North
    American Decoys

Harold Haertel

Larry Hayden

The Reverend Jack Drake

Gilbert Maggioni

Arnold Melbye

William Koelpin

Lynn Forehand

Doug Miller

Andy Andrews

Gary Yoder

Kenneth Basile

Robert Phinney

Larry Barth

Floyd Scholz

Marcus Schultz

Robert Guge

Jerry Barkley

Habbart Dean

Ernest Muehlmatt

Curtis Badger *for* Wildfowl Art,
    journal of the Ward Foundation

Kenneth Scheeler

"Nothing caught him the way carving did."

John and I were always close, even though there were six children in our family. We were only two years apart. I would describe him as an average kid, getting into a little mischief now and then. We had a great time together. When it came to activities, John liked sports, football, and hunting.

Just before World War II, he got his first car and he would go to the local river and catch snapping turtles. He'd go under a bridge and grab them by the tails when they swam by. He loved that kind of life, but nothing caught him the way carving did.

Our dad was a house painter, and I was a house painter, but John started out as a mechanic, something he learned in the service. After the war, he got married and we went to Atlantic City and painted hotel exteriors. He found he could make more money painting than being a mechanic.

Then he went into business for himself and for several years painted Bell Telephone buildings. He kept his business small, just wanting to make a comfortable living.

But despite his early career as a mechanic, he always had a painting background. He did some still lifes. One I remember was a watermelon sitting on newspaper. I think this flatwork art helped him with the painting of his carvings.

Our father, in fact, did some sign painting at one time, making posters and signs for trucks. But he had no carving ability.

At one time John and I worked together as painters. He did some carving then, and I remember one time he came to work and told me he saw an article in a magazine about a man carving birds professionally. "Wouldn't that be something if you could carve for a living?" John said. He never dreamed that a few years down the road he would be doing just that.

When John got started carving, he didn't really know what was going on. A friend of his told him about this bird carving show in Salisbury, Maryland. He went there and got all fired up. He saw the Reverend Drake's work, particularly a preening dove, and he couldn't get over the workmanship.

After that, he decided he wanted to visit the Wards and asked me to go with him to Crisfield, Maryland, where the Wards lived. He said a man who owned a sporting goods store in Maine and another fellow, Jim West, who was a decoy carver, were going along. We saw Lem and Steve and had a great time talking to them, then went to visit a collector of antique decoys in Cambridge, Maryland. Jim sold him an old Ward decoy for a hundred dollars, which was, no doubt, a good buy.

After John started carving, I became interested in decoys and he suggested I try carving birds. That was in 1970. I worked with him in his shop and soon got my own tools and worked at my own house. But periodically, maybe once a week, I would go over to John's place and find him carving out in the shop. He said he heard about a show on Long Island called the U.S. National Decoy Show. Again, he asked me to go along. The following year I went there and took a first- and third-place ribbon with canvasbacks. The next year I made a scaup for the amateur division. This was awarded Best in Show. Later I made an oldsquaw for the World Competition. The judges said the neck wasn't right. I took it home and did some painting on it and told John I was going into the professional class at a show in Mississippi. John simply said, do what you want. The bird took a Best in Show. It was a good start, and I've won Best in Shows here and there.

John was a motivating force behind my carving. And whenever I went to see him, I'd take a carving I thought was nice. Then I'd see something he did, want to improve my bird, and come back to my shop and work, even before I went into the house.

One thing I remember was that he would never carve when someone besides me was around. I always liked company, but he would put the tools down when someone else was there. In the last years he would put the tools aside even when I visited him, and we'd end up looking at his flower beds or going to a nearby wildlife sanctuary to see some waterfowl.

The beginning years as a carver were not easy for him. When he first quit his painting business and carved full time, he didn't do too well. He was getting $175 for a decoy. Then Doug Miller suggested that John work for him. From then on it was like going to school and getting paid for it. He could take a piece and spend as much time on it as he wanted and perfect it to the best of his ability and even send it to a show. He couldn't have done that if he hadn't been working for someone. Some carvers told John that he could make more money working for himself, but John wasn't that aggressive. He was content taking the route he took. Later he worked for Andy Andrews, since John thought it would be good to make a change.

When John started entering competitions, when ducks were working decoys, John's birds were almost too decorative. But it wasn't long before the competitions started accepting decorative waterfowl. I remember a scaup he took to the U.S. National Decoy Show. He got a blue ribbon right away with it, and this was the first time he had ever entered a floating decoy.

John put a lot of character into his early decorative decoys, though, seen super close, they don't look like the birds being done

Ken Scheeler, John's brother, well remembers the character John put into his early waterfowl, especially the heads. This is a canvasback hen. In the collection of Andy and Sandy Andrews.

today. You can look at the work of a wildfowl painter and you see how super neat the details are. But look at another painter's work, and it's altogether different. There may be a richness that the other paintings don't have. I picture John's ducks the same way. Though they weren't so finely done, they had character. And John was not a copier. He came up with original ideas. For example, he would carve a head and put a lot of work under it on the breast, giving it a nice shape.

I have to say, though, that my favorite piece is not a duck but a goshawk and crow, one of his very best pieces. I also like his pair of grouse composition for its action. It was a funny thing about those grouse. He came up with the idea and then a taxidermist mounted a pair the way John carved them. One day the father-in-law of the taxidermist came over to John's house and pointed out to his son-in-law that John had copied his grouse. The father-in-law was quickly corrected.

John had a great imagination for getting action into pieces and making birds look lifelike. He told me once that a lot of carvers did neater work than he did and that he just couldn't come up with super clean birds. But if you stepped back a few feet, they had the look that many of those carvers couldn't capture.

The surf scoters he really labored over. He even used a live bird as a model when he was painting them. But what came easy were the rocks and stones and shells he would do for a composition like that one.

Ken adds that John was not a copier. He developed his own style.

The little sparrow hawk on one leg is also a favorite of mine. He worked right through on that, with little effort. Some birds he labored on, remaking them. But sometimes he would make one and it would fall right into place.

John was an innovator in other ways. I know that he was the one who really got people started with the Foredom. A man John knew had carved some horses; they were beautifully done. Someone said he learned to do them in prison. But whatever the story, he did them with a Foredom. So when John got interested in carving, he grabbed a Foredom and even took one to the Wards. Everyone was amazed at what could be done with this tool.

As for inserting feathers, he picked that up from Gilbert Maggioni, but at times he complained about doing inserts, saying he wanted to get back to basic carving. In fact, the last bird he made, his peregrine falcon, was basically one piece. I think, too, you are better off without all the inserts. I just think one-piece work makes for better carving.

John contributed a lot in terms of design and composition, but his special contribution was the look of the birds. I think they were in a class by themselves because of that. He could get a look to his hawks. I call it the character of a bird. A lot of carvers would make birds that looked more like decoys than birds. But John would put in lumps and bumps to bring out the character. I think he was a master at that.

He also contributed to the field of bird carving by the way he challenged others. I think competition is a great motivating force. Without competitions, carving would never be where it is today. I believe it's the competitions that drive you on. When I see people who drop out of competition, I feel sorry for them. Some of those carvers say that they have nothing more to gain because they have won all the important events, but then they have a tendency to relax and not live up to their potential. John, I know, was a physical wreck before the shows, and after the shows he felt good. On the outside he was quiet, but competitions got him worked up inside. Still, he turned out great pieces, and I think that was due to the competitions.

Julius Iski

"His work had a flair, an artistry, even in the beginning."

I used to paint, a Sunday painter, you might say. But I met Jimmy West, an old-time decoy maker, and when I saw his work, I started carving. The first birds I ever made, a pair of buffleheads, won Best in Show at the U.S. National Decoy Show in 1969. That was held in Babylon, New York.

We were using Dremel tools and bits to texture the surface, but there was no burning until later. I raised primaries on my birds, but there was little insertion work at the time.

Julius Iski is a pioneer in the carving of decorative decoys. Iski recalls that Scheeler did not accept feather insertion until he did a flying black duck. In the collection of the Wildlife World Museum.

I first met John at Smithville, New Jersey, in 1969. Yearly exhibits were held there. John went to a lot of shows after that. I won the first World Championship in 1971 with a pair of oldsquaw. John went to that contest with a pair of geese. He felt bad about not taking a ribbon. The judges apparently thought the geese were a little too small. What bothered him was that he had sold the geese and thought they were worth a ribbon. That was the first big show for him.

The shows were not unlike the ones today except that there was little money involved. Carvers went for ribbons, though the World Championships offered prize money. My oldsquaw won $500.

After seeing what John was doing, I couldn't wait until the following year to see what he came up with. His work had a flair, an artistry, even in the beginning. There was something about it that caught the eye. As he progressed he expanded on his own ideas to where he got to be when he died.

Early on he picked up the techniques of texturing, then burning, then inserts. At first he didn't accept insertions, but I remember a flying black duck he brought to the U.S. National Decoy Show. That had separate feathers.

As for myself, I quit carving for about nine years. John kept after me to get back to it, which I am doing now. It will take someone great to fill his shoes.

Byron Cheever for
North American Decoys

"He seems to have found his ultimate means of self-expression by painting on wood."

When it comes to decoys and wildlife carvings, there is one thing you can be sure of and that is change. Tools, techniques and painting media coupled with the ingenuity of the individual carvers and sparked by a spirit of competition, have each played their part. One idea which has received wide acclaim is that of texturing the bird prior to painting. The "smoothies," as Roger Barton calls them, are out. Not that the old collectors' items finished with barn or boat paint are any less desirable, nor is it likely that the excellent contemporary birds painted over a smoothly sanded surface will be tossed aside. These are all hard won treasures and will be treated accordingly, but even the old decoy makers found some pleasure in a textured surface, which they achieved by stippling, combing and ornate wing and feather carving.

An early magazine article about Scheeler says that the secret of his success lay with his ability to "condition the wood and texture the bird prior to painting." This is an early canvasback drake. In the collection of Andy and Sandy Andrews.

One of the first men to give this idea a modern touch was John Scheeler of Mays Landing, New Jersey. The name New Jersey might lead you to believe that John had grown up in a decoy maker's shop, but this is not the case. In fact, he is a relative newcomer to the art of bird carving. John's interest was sparked by a visit to the Wildfowl Carving and Arts Exhibit in Salisbury, Maryland. He entered the hall as a casual observer and left with a resolve to try his hand with a knife and brush.

The results were good. So good that John was able to win top honors in both decorative and working pairs divisions at the 1972 contest in Salisbury.

Whenever he carved, he always turned out his birds in pairs, including both male and female of the species. The pairs competition was a natural for him. He preferred to carve diving ducks, the widgeon being a favorite. With his initial effort at Salisbury, he won 3rd place, having previously achieved "Best of Show" earlier in the year with a pair of decorative widgeons at the U.S. National Decoy Contest, Babylon, New York.

His mergansers, "Best of Show" working pairs, are shown with the photographic coverage of the 1972 World Championship Wildfowl Carving Competition in an issue of NAD, and his beautiful pair of sparrow hawks, which took top honors in the decorative pairs, are pictured here.

The secret of John's success lies in his unusual ability to condition the wood and texture the bird prior to painting. This is achieved with a small power tool with a flexible shaft, and rotary drills, some of his own design. The result is a pleasing softness and naturalness in the feather pattern and finished carving. By emphasizing this particular part of the work, let us take nothing away from John's ability as a painter. He paints with oils and does a masterful job. A self-employed industrial painter, John took art lessons for about 6 months and did some oil painting, but he seems to have found his ultimate means of self-expression by painting on wood rather than canvas.

One other item that helped to bring John almost instant recognition was his ability to capture the birds in natural and lifelike positions. This is a part of the carving process that sometimes gives would-be carvers much difficulty. John was no doubt helped in this regard by the fact that he kept a few tame mallards in his back yard and had ample opportunity to observe them. He also kept a freezer, originally intended for food, well stocked with frozen waterfowl, which he used for study and inspiration in his work. Even with this help, however, there must be a certain inherent talent involved that enabled John to see the birds as they really are and transmit this naturalness into each of his carvings.

John used copper and canvas for the legs and feet on his birds and except for the contest decoys, most of his work consisted of full-bodied birds in a sitting or preening position attractively displayed on select pieces of driftwood. Having a constant urge to improve, John found ways to build upon a well-established reputation as a carver of wooden birds.

—Reprinted from 1972 issue of *North American Decoys*

Harold Haertel

"He was responsible for the biggest change in carving."

I made my first decoy out of the ends of an orange crate. It was a floating profile, and I was twelve at the time. I made it with a scroll saw and colored it with ink. I floated it in the Fox River near my home in Dundee, Illinois, and I had never seen a decoy in my life at the time. I was calling, and a bird swam within a yard of the decoy.

I always enjoyed making decoys. Early on they were bluebills, mallards, black ducks, pintails. In the 1920s I made bluebills, but I never made decoys to sell.

I was concerned with attitudes. One of the best attractors of them all is a high-neck decoy. Another is a bird with its bill in the water. These were attitudes that worked well in this river.

Of course, I never saw John carve. And he was always kind of bashful and quiet. But I figured that he was responsible for the biggest change in carving since he started carving. It was his working with different types of tools and making carvings more lifelike. Burning, grinding, and inserts made his work quite a departure from what I do.

I don't burn, and the only time I use a Foredom is on the heads of birds. I do an entirely different type of carving, working almost entirely with a knife and rasp. I don't go for inserting, either. I make a decoy and fancy it up. I don't try to make a realistic bird.

When I judged in Salisbury, John had a pair of goldeneyes. That was in 1971. He didn't have them weighted right. They were leaning, though the carving was real good. The heads were thrust forward quite a bit, and if you don't have that counterbalanced, you end up with a lopsided floating bird. He lost because of that.

Everyone had a lot of respect for him because he was responsible for a lot of improvement in bird carving.

Larry Hayden

"His birds projected so dramatically that the painting was secondary."

My background includes painting, illustrating, and duck carving, and I helped introduce burning for texturing. The first time I met John was the year of the first Ward Foundation competition, in 1971. It was also the year I started carving. I went there as a nobody and had taken one blue ribbon at a Michigan show before that. But I brought four decoys to Maryland. There used to be bleachers by the sides of the flotation tanks. I was sitting there next to this fellow I didn't know. We started talking about the show, and that was the year pairs were entered. We were talking about decoys other than our own. I said, "Do you see that beautiful pair of goldeneyes on the table?" He said yes and added that they were his. He introduced himself as John Scheeler. Incidentally, his pair won a blue ribbon, as did all four of my ducks.

I had been using a wood burner at the time of the early World shows, and John was using a Foredom tool for texturing. Quite often we get satisfied with our tools. He was selling Foredoms for someone, and he said I ought to buy one. I said to myself, I don't need one of them. I can get by with just wood burning. As it turned out, I won Best in Show that year and some prize money, so I figured I had to spend it. I gave in and bought a Foredom, figuring I would never use it, that I'd leave it on my shelf as a decoration for visitors to see. But the next year I did use it, and it's one of the tools I use so much that I ask myself how I ever carved without it. That's the memory I recall the most when thinking about John.

Over the years he would call me if he found a new brush or new brand of paint. Or he would call and say he had trouble achieving this color or that and ask me if I had any ideas. Many of our conversations went like that.

I have a canvasback John carved. I think it is typical of the decoys John used to make. He accented the character, especially in the head. That's why his birds appealed to me so much. One of the most important things when a bird is being judged, particularly a decoy, is

Larry Hayden, another pioneer in the art of the decorative decoy, says that Scheeler's ducks projected the character of the species. This is a gadwall drake Scheeler did in the early 1970s. In the collection of the Wildlife World Museum.

the likeness to the species of the bird. If a decoy doesn't project the character of the bird, the rest, the painting and carving, is superficial.

I think, then, that his painting style was secondary to his carving. His birds projected so dramatically that the painting was secondary. It was only a color on his carvings. They were so strongly carved, they almost didn't need to be painted. Some other carvings would be lost without the painting because it carries the carving.

I look at John's work as sculpture. His methods were so different from the way I carve: I use tight patterns, but his works came as much from his mind and hands as they did from patterns.

John did a lot to promote carving. He was a goodwill ambassador. It's easy to promote carving if you're promoting yourself, but that was not the case with John. He never went around bragging about his achievements. Instead, he always brought people's attention to the better carvings; it didn't matter who carved them.

John was so unselfish, introducing me to other carvers or collectors. These are things he didn't have to do. I remember that first year, when I won with a pintail drake. Lem Ward was still alive. He was an idol of mine, someone I wouldn't have even thought to introduce myself to. He came around and saw my bird and wanted to meet me. It was John who brought him over.

John also had a keen interest in maintaining the integrity of the carving field. If something was going on that he didn't think was right, he would try to correct it. He wanted to maintain high standards.

John could do this because he had the exposure. He attended shows all around the country. He even came to the North American Wildfowl Carving Championship here in Michigan. He would travel to California to compete. Other carvers tended to be local. But John became nationally known.

When you first enter a competition, you're not as pressured and can sit back and have fun, but if you start winning, people expect you to keep entering and winning. John had the same problem I had. We both built a reputation. You're expected not just to enter but also to win. That puts a heavy burden on you, and John entered a lot longer than I did. After a while you're not glad that you won, you're glad you didn't lose. I think John felt that way.

Nonetheless, the best years of my carving career were when John and I went to shows and we were both entering. He entered decoys in the beginning and we would sit in the bleachers and try to pick the winners in divisions we didn't have a bird in.

Few carvers in my lifetime will have a niche in the development of bird carving. Lem Ward will be one of them. And John Scheeler will be another.

The Reverend Jack Drake

"You can't complain if you've won the
Best-in-World title."

Most of the bird carvers have come into the field through someone else. My entry was original, and I've been told that I have done more to put bird carving into its present realm than anyone else.

When I started bird carving, I didn't know anyone else who did this. I had heard about the Ward brothers, whom I met before they passed away. They were known for their decoys, but they had not really gone into decorative bird carving. So I did this on my own for years.

I carved my first birds when I was sixteen or seventeen. They were miniature birds. That was in the 1930s. The first life-size bird I did, a sparrow, was in 1943.

I was a pioneer in the burning technique, starting with what was called the burning pencil. It burned details in plaques. I redesigned the point of an Unger wood-burning pencil, making my own tips and filing them. There was no one who was carving in feather detail before I started wood burning.

This came from a meeting with an Arizona woodcarver named Jack Pence. He was using a wood-burning pencil to put some detail into wood. But he said you can't burn a bird. It's too far out. That was about 1963.

I have yet to pick up a new burning tool that allows you to change the temperature of the heat. I'd like to get one for certain details. I still use an Unger soldering iron.

Maggioni and McKoy and later John got into burning when the Baker Gallery of Lubbock, Texas, brought some of my work to Salisbury in 1969. All the carvers there said they had never seen work like that. When I went to Salisbury the following year, people told me I had revolutionized the exhibition. I said how could I have? I had never been there before. They told me they had never seen work like this. Then Maggioni began to do insertions of feathers for wings and tails. I've done a little of that, but most of the wing spreads I make consist of one piece and each feather is done in that block.

For separating the feathers, I still use a knife, though I have changed from a Dremel to a Foredom for detailing. And I switched from oils to acrylics about 1972.

I met the Ward brothers in 1968 when I went to Maryland for a meeting, dropped in on them and got acquainted with both. In fact, I have a letter from Lem saying that I had reached the highest level in this profession of bird carving. That was quite a compliment.

The only time I met John was in 1973. He had entered a competition with a peregrine falcon and a green-winged teal. I walked over and looked at this carving and told John, whom I had just met, that it was a nice piece of work. He said, yes, but it needs some improvement. I said you can't complain if you've won the Best-in-World title. He responded by saying that he wouldn't have won if my work and Maggioni's and McKoy's had been there. I said that remains to be seen. That was the only time we met.

About that time I did a pioneer project that has two mockingbirds, one in flight. It is supported by a flower stem, which comes up and makes contact with a metal leg. One of my finest carvings is a pair of scissortail flycatchers with an iris in bloom. My work has been displayed at the White House, and I did a pair of passenger pigeons for the Smithsonian Institution in Washington.

I have been asked why I do compositions with flowers. My answer is that the type of work you do depends on whom you're trying to impress. If you're impressing rugged men, you do hawks or birds in combat and anger. If you're pleasing the ladies, you have to have the delicate touch with flowers. So since I was doing my birds to sell, I wanted to impress both ladies and men and decided on flowers.

I never did the kind of compositions Maggioni and McKoy do. I remember Maggioni's peregrine falcon swooping down through rushes on three green-winged teals. The suspension work was superb. But that kind of work is impressive to those who are used to hunting or seeing birds in the wild, swooping down on things. This was not the case with me.

Gilbert Maggioni

"Strange that a person so gentle and mild
in his nature should have such a rapt admiration
of the fiercest bird in nature."

I went on a goose-hunting trip to Kent County in Maryland in 1967, I believe. During the course of that visit, I went to a bird carving exhibit held under the auspices of the local Audubon society in Chestertown. That was the first exposure I had to that art form. I didn't know too much about it, though I had been exposed to some decoy carving, having been a duck hunter. I had made my own decoys, had experience in woodworking, but I never saw this type of carving or presentation.

Several things impressed me about that show. One was that although the work was beautifully done and painted and you could see that realism and naturalism were the ultimate aim of the carvers, the carvers were not exploiting the medium to the extent that they could have. Very few birds were shown with uplifted wings; also, there were few birds in flight. That struck me as being backward, really. Why weren't they showing birds in flight? I came home and got started with bird carving.

The first time I showed my work was in Salisbury in 1969. I was told that several of the carvers who exhibited in Chestertown were also in Salisbury. Arnold Melbye was one of them, and the Ward brothers were there.

It was in 1970 that I met John Scheeler. With the advent of the Ward show more people became interested in bird carving, though until then I doubt that more than fifty people were carving decorative birds full time. It was an early stage of bird carving.

In searching back through my memory, I have the distinct impression that whenever there was a discussion among the carvers at the exhibition, the primary topic was technique and procedure. I'm sure that John discussed these things enthusiastically. One of the prominent things I remember about him is his constant search to improve his work technically. Acrylic paints had just become available, and they solved a lot of problems. But I don't believe there was a lot of exploration of design. Most of the carvers were perfectly content to lift a design from Audubon or Fuertes. That was my impression. And most of the carved birds were perched very statically on a piece of driftwood.

At the same time I started to explore the possibilities of flying birds, which soon turned out to be nearly impossible because of the nature of the wood, the end grain. I just couldn't handle it. To carve a bent wing in flight out of a solid block, that was a quixotic effort. So I hit upon the method of using pieces of wood as individual feathers. These could be carved individually and twisted to whatever shape was required and then inserted into a basic wing made out of carved, solid wood.

I took such a bird to my first show, one with individually inserted feathers. That was the direction I was going in. At the same time, once you did a bird carving, you had the tremendous problem of how to display it logically. You couldn't very well hang it from a piece of piano wire. So that led to the development of habitat and how to put the bird in the air sensibly and credibly so that the average person coming along would say that this is a bird taking off or a bird landing. And most positions in flight had to be near the ground.

The following year a fellow from New Mexico sent the Ward Foundation exhibition some birds on which the feathers were textured. The barb lines had been burned into the wood. That was the first blush of attention to barb lines. A lot of conjecture ensued as to how the burning was done. Someone came up with the idea that it was done with a soldering iron. Everyone went out and bought soldering irons. John, of course, was vitally interested in all these conversations.

John had a fixation with the raptors. He did this subject repeatedly, and with prey. Each time he did it markedly better, radically improving his technique. I found it rather strange that a person so gentle and mild in his nature should have such a rapt admiration of the fiercest bird in nature. That always impressed me about John. But he never would clarify my curiosity on the subject.

And what is John's place in the history of carving? I have a problem with that question. If you look at his position within the context of the competitions, then certainly he is preeminent. But my problem is that many of those competitions are mass media arrangements, not meant to encourage fine art. I have turned it over in my mind, and I find that John may have done himself a disservice by maintaining that long connection with contests. He might have done better had he concentrated on exhibiting in museums. And if he had made some connection with a top-drawer gallery, he might have increased his stature. He had the ability to do it. Grainger McKoy did just such a thing.

I think that John was not an aggressor. He was the reverse of that, which may have worked against him, though not in my estimation. But it may have worked against his stature as an artist.

Fine art doesn't necessarily become finer with democratization. Early on I recommended that exhibitions jury all work before accepting it. Today you have to cope with the intense commercialization of wildlife art and the mediocrity of it. When something becomes highly commercial, mistakes proliferate.

I would like to add that woodcarving is not in its infancy. This wrong-end-of-the-telescope concentration on birds in woodcarving is not a healthy thing. We have seen contests and carving exhibitions spring up all over the country. We've seen this tremendous upsurge in interest that borders on the fad classification, and might not fall far short of a craze. We've seen the number of bird carvers go out of the stratosphere. I think this is an unhealthy sign for what should be a basic thing. I can't understand how a perfectly qualified woodcarver can limit himself to birds. There are so many other things to carve and things that lend themselves to the wonderful new technology of burning, acrylic paint, and power tools we have now. The whole concentration on birds is myopic, it seems to me.

What we are doing in bird carving is employing high-tech technique to approach a degree of realism that hasn't been approached in carving before, but we are restricting it to birds. A friend of mine had been to the Baseball Hall of Fame in Cooperstown, New York. There was a life-size statue of Babe Ruth in batting position carved in wood by Rhode Island sculptor Armand LaMontagne. The details, my friend said, were remarkable. It's difficult, then, for me to gauge the position of one man in a very narrow area of one art form.

As for myself, I quit carving in 1975. There were personal and business reasons. I had to get out for a number of years, but when I got back in, the spark was gone. And it hasn't returned. The last year I exhibited in Salisbury was 1975. But I returned twice to judge the World Championship and I visited the Ward exhibition in 1981. That was the last time I saw John. I'm out of touch with what he did after 1981. He used to call me several times a year, and we talked about various techniques.

I have been asked why I did such animated poses. Wildlife is in a constant state of tension between prey and predator, between the dominated and the dominator. I think drama derives from those tensions. The stoop of a peregrine falcon is one of the most dramatic incidents in wildlife. I think the feeding frenzy of bluefish, never tackled by an artist, is brutal but natural. Carvers today have drifted too far from that naturalism. Everything has to be nice and sugary. If we could learn from the natural world, we wouldn't be so inclined to accept unnatural situations in our lives, and the western world would be much stronger for it.

Arnold Melbye

"He knew what he was after."

In my early youth I learned how to draw. My father would bring home a duck and let me examine it, so I got to handle and draw birds at a very early age. And what I couldn't draw, my mother, who was an artist in her own right, helped me sketch.

An uncle who was a carpenter and an avid hunter always brought me something when he visited. He would bring birds and other animals he had shot. I would put them down on paper and even make drawings of the wings. I also made paper birds, cutouts, that I flew from an upstairs landing.

Much later, in the 1930s, I met Elmer Crowell and saw his work. He did pleasing birds. He had a style of his own, and there was no question about what bird he was doing. I had made my own hunting decoys, and I told my wife that I wanted to try some decorative carving. When I built the house in 1940 that I'm still in, I set up shop in a small ell that is now my kitchen.

In 1965 I attended the first American Bird Carving Exhibit in Chestertown, Maryland. I attended the two other biennial shows, and in 1968 I cut the ribbon with Lem and Steve Ward for the first Atlantic Flyway Exhibition, which was to become the Ward Foundation show.

In 1971 the Easton Waterfowl Festival started, and that's where I met John. He had ducks on his table, not working decoys but decorative waterfowl. They were wonderful. They caught the birds. It was obvious that he had studied them. On many of the early carved waterfowl, the heads and bills were too wide and the heads were fat. But John had trimmed his birds down to what they really are. His canvasback had a real head on it. That's what impressed me and caught my eye even from a distance.

I could see from where I was sitting that the birds John had on his table were something I wanted to see at close range. So I went over to look at them and I said hello to him. But he wasn't exactly talkative. I said, "For what it's worth, I think those are the finest

Arnold Melbye, an early influence on Scheeler, believes a key to his friend's success was a profound understanding of bird anatomy. Melbye is particularly impressed with Scheeler's goshawk and crow. He points out that the hawk's forward leg is carrying the weight. In the collection of the North American Wildfowl Art Museum.

ducks I've seen in a long time." I knew my ducks because that was all I had been doing for years. He was very modest, but I knew he felt good about having someone notice his work. He later brought his birds to the Audubon show in Fairfield, Connecticut.

Marshall Case, who was in charge of this Audubon unit, asked me to contact the carvers for a show, knowing I was acquainted with most of them. I wrote endless letters that winter, and my wife typed them all. I was delighted when John called saying that he would come. He continued to call me after that.

But I really spent very little time with him, since I stopped going to shows when they became too commercial. They got so crowded you couldn't see anything. I did visit the Wards, and I might have

Melbye finds artistically pleasing the complementary curves of the hawk's and the crow's wings. He says Scheeler was able to create such depth with his paints that the viewer would have trouble telling whether a feather was carved or only painted.

visited John, but my wife got sick, and I had to take care of her for five years. But when we talked on the telephone, it was about new tools, painting, lighting. He even sent me tools to try. He was very generous that way.

We also talked about what was going on in the carving world. I'm so isolated here on the Cape. The only show I go to is the Fairfield show, and that's because there are no merchandisers.

I work with bird skins and measure everything and try to get the proportions right. I know that John was smart enough to get good mounts. If you have something like that, and you know your business, you're in good shape. Raptors are hard to get, but John had friends who would give him mounts.

You usually don't get a mount in the position you've decided to carve the bird in. How did he get the motion he wanted? You would have thought he drew, but he didn't. Right from the beginning, then, he knew what he was after.

Take that goshawk and crow he did. You can see how he has all the weight on the hawk's forward leg. He also has the wings curved down and the crow's wings curved back up. Even the goshawk's tail has good symmetry, done as if by an architect. Those elements bring the whole piece together. I think John had good common sense besides being an artist.

He was versatile as a carver. He did a pair of ruffed grouse. I think he must have had a photograph of these birds. I've hunted a lot of grouse, so I like the life he has in them. He has the oak leaves flying around. When one of those birds takes off in an oak grove, it will kick leaves up as much as four feet. You have that action in the piece.

John told me that he got nervous when it came to doing songbirds. They were too small. He didn't like to work with such small objects. I could see his point. You can see and correct errors in a large piece that you can't necessarily see in a small one. I measure things on songbird skins down to one sixty-fourth of an inch. But you don't have to be quite that accurate with large birds.

With his painting he learned to blend. It's hard to blend acrylics. Looking at the feathers on the goshawk, you don't know whether they're there by carving or by painting. John could create that look just with painting, using a dark, a medium, and a light color.

I think John was a master who inspired other top carvers. He made birds others could go by.

William Koelpin

"When we talked, we saw eye to eye on a lot of things."

My first involvement with John was through Douglas Miller. I always felt I got Miller interested in bird carving, though I don't know whether he will back me up on that. But whatever the case, when I met him, he knew little about the bird art form, though he may have collected paintings and decoys. I told him that this was a new art form in North America and that it was going places. I also explained that it was unique because of the decoy heritage and described how decorative carving was evolving from that. He evidently was impressed by the carvings he was seeing. He decided that he would become a collector and a patron.

I assume I was the first carver who signed a contract with him. That was in 1971. John was the second and William Schultz was the third.

The first time I saw John's work I was in complete awe of it. It was magnificent. Those were the days when we relied more on the painted surface than on the textured surface to get our point across. Today more detailed carving is done to convey the essence of a bird. Back then we did relatively smooth birds. John's painting ability was phenomenal. I looked at his painting and was dumbfounded by the accuracy and realism, yet it was an effect. John was an impressionistic painter.

William Koelpin feels that most carved flying birds are not successful because the action is stopped dead. Scheeler's birds, he says, seem to move. Koelpin is also impressed with Scheeler's painting style, which he describes as impressionistic. In the collection of the Wildlife World Museum.

If you looked at the individual feathers he did, you found that they were painted very loosely. They weren't finely rendered. In some cases it looked as though he had used an old, split-haired brush to get the effects of feathering. The feathers were loose, then, made with gusto and broad, sweeping brush strokes. Yet there was still a delicate realism to them.

I think bird painting is a lot stronger with this strategy because the birds tend to project over a distance more than those made with one-haired brush strokes. John would take a major feather group and do it with three, four, five sweeps of the brush. He made his own realism, which you sometimes have to do when working with the mediums of wood and paint. You simply can't make a real feather out of wood and paint.

I remember seeing John's birds in Miller's collection. I used to pick up his birds, both decoy and decorative, and find that the painting under the bellies or under the tails or on the legs was more beautiful than on other areas. John tended to loosen up there and paint even more impressionistically. That was something because we tend to overlook the underneath parts. But John later changed his style and did better overall with his painting.

Another thing that impressed me was the anatomy of John's birds. They had movement. He could twist the bird around and make it come alive. That was extraordinary even back in the early 1970s, when I first got to know his work. All of a sudden a carver had come up with anatomically correct birds, and the only way he could have done that was by understanding bird anatomy. A lot of neophyte carvers today are trying to do something that they don't understand. They're not learning basic bird anatomy.

Another contribution of John's was in making birds that were rarely carved. Working with Doug Miller, we had access to more exotic species through museums and private collections. John immediately jumped in and started doing some of the unusual species, primarily raptors.

But he did other outstanding birds. I remember a flying willet he did. He had that ability to make a bird look as though it were flying. I've seen flying birds attempted so often, and they usually end up as flops. The flying bird has tremendous action and speed, and the carver is stopping it dead. But John could get the relaxed feeling that the bird was flying across the table. That was amazing.

With John's encouragement I went ahead and did things other people were afraid to try or thought weren't right to do. I did a life-size great blue heron when birds that big or of that species weren't being done. And I probably did birds that I couldn't handle artistically, but I also tried upland gamebirds, such as pheasants and prairie chickens, and put them in their environments.

And I did different things like staining wood, and I was probably one of the first carvers to take off and say I would be a professional bird carver before retiring.

Though John and I never socialized much, even when we both worked for Miller, John used to call me quite a bit. I looked forward to his calls, which came about once a month. He seemed to enjoy them. When we talked, we saw eye to eye on a lot of things. One of them was making birds project without a lot of rendering. John understood fine art and sculpture. I don't know whether he had any formal schooling in those areas, but I'm sure that at some point he studied great sculpture and great paintings. Many times we would talk about simplicity. So many carving compositions tended to get complicated, with so many different elements in them, but if we looked at a John Scheeler bird, we'd ask ourselves why we didn't think of taking his approach. For John had the ability to see things simply. All great art is based on simplicity. Complicated, garish things, no matter how well they're done, don't constitute art. Simplicity John understood, in design and composition. He let nothing detract from the main element, which naturally is the bird in this art form.

Yet you could look at some of his pieces and visualize a whole forest floor, and he'd have only a single element. He had the ability to capture the essence of a forest floor or a marsh with a simple object or very little material.

A lot of times John would talk about something he saw that he thought was really great, and surprisingly, it wasn't a wood carving. He'd talk about some painting, perhaps a Robert Bateman painting. He would mention how he envied the abilities of people like Bateman. That surprised me because he had the ability beyond any carver I knew.

He would talk about Robert Phinney, an artist he knew who did bronzes, and ask me why I didn't do more bronzes. But now I'm getting back to them, and John may have been responsible for that.

He often told me that he wanted to work in clay and make a bronze from it. I believe he could have done some spectacular things. But I can't imagine that he didn't at least once take a piece of clay or wax and make something. I do know that John made study models out of Styrofoam and clay.

We would talk about what we didn't like about carving, the mechanical aspects of it that make the birds look all the same, such as overburning. Some people overtexture to disguise bad painting or overpaint to disguise bad surfaces. John never did that.

At one time we were in heated but friendly competition, but I never got the feeling that I was in direct competition with him. One of us winning made it all right. With John you knew there'd be tremendous competition, but you didn't get the feeling that you lost if he won. I think that's an amazing attribute.

He was a private individual who hated the limelight. He was proud and wanted to win. How else could he have been in the competitions year after year? I think he wanted to win for himself and the satisfaction of making something that was his best effort. That, too, is a great attribute.

Certainly he had an ego—you have to have one to be an artist—

but it was a private ego. He was fighting himself and trying to prove his ability to himself. That's probably why he never said anything negative about a particular carver. He'd only talk about good or bad work. Only if a great piece was involved would he mention a name. He had tremendous character.

Lynn Forehand

"When it came to carvings, he could see good
in every piece, even at competitions."

At a time when you might have been competing against him, John Scheeler would call you up and encourage you. When I was doing the jungle fowl that won The World in 1979, I was at the point where I would sleep one night and work the next. I would hurt physically, and I had thoughts of quitting. But John must have been psychic because the phone would ring, and it was John saying you can't quit now. You can do it. He did not compete that year, not having finished his flying ruffed grouse. But if he had, he would still have been on the phone encouraging me. Many other carvers have not encouraged competition.

John was all for the art form. You don't always have that with new carvers. In what I call the old days, everyone was on the phone helping each other.

The 1970s in particular were a time of experimentation, with carvers living in different parts of the country, working in isolation for a while. But it was at the competitions that we started to exchange ideas. Things were happening, and this communication is why bird carving evolved as rapidly as it did. For example, I was staining pieces back then, but they were coming out rough. I tried putting lacquer on the wood, and then I put a rotary bristle brush in my Foredom and hit the lacquer. It slicked the wood as smooth as glass. And I realized that lacquer is a good foundation for acrylic paints. I shared that with John, who liked the results when he tried it. This is the way changes take place.

We were all experimenters in the 1970s because we had no books and everything was so new. But the newness meant we had a whole world of choices. Even the grinding and texturing tools evolved from experimentation.

I remember that John was experimenting with the crow under the goshawk. He told me he was fed up with painting it. He went down to the hardware store, bought a can of Rustoleum spray paint, went home and used it. Later he said the crow came out perfect.

We also experimented with conflict, and we were accused of doing birds that were violent. But I don't consider nature violent. I think any violence in nature stems from a need to survive. It happens because it is necessary.

Another thing that came out of the 1970s was flying birds, and John and I both did them. Pieces like my three doves coming out of a cornfield are difficult to move, so you don't do many of them. But I liked the challenge of getting them up in the air.

With that composition, my thinking was for a pleasing piece that would look good from every angle. John took the same approach with his flying terns. That's the challenge of working in the round rather than working on a canvas. It has to look good from all angles. And when it's displayed, it's usually placed so that you can walk around it and see it from all angles.

But birds in the air are very difficult to achieve, and the higher you go, the heavier the birds become. You braze metal together, but as the height increases, a tremendous strain is put on the pieces. So you have to achieve balance without the birds looking stiff. And you don't want the piece to fall apart ten or twenty years later.

All this has to do with feeling the composition. Without question, John had a feeling for what he was doing. Sometimes I think he really became the piece he was working on. I don't see any way he could have achieved what he did without that happening.

John told me many times to keep a piece simple, keep it plain. You can still have all the appeal you need. Birds in flight are great, he said, but often they're flashy. They can appear overdone. I believe he preferred to do just a standing bird. I think he tackled in-flight birds for the challenge. But a standing or sitting bird can be just as appealing, depending on the pose and the expression established.

John and I talked about everything from religion to types of wood. Sometimes at shows we would sit in his car, drink coffee, and talk about birds. When it came to other carvers, John never talked about them unless what he said was good. And when it came to carvings, he could see good in every piece, even at competitions.

John was an average person, although some people put him in a category beyond that. He was an ordinary person who worked for a living and made a living at this, one of the few who could.

What helped in the early years was Doug Miller. He helped establish a price for what we were doing, and he was the first person to pay big money. He saw a future in this and started buying. He gave me a financial jolt by buying a few big pieces. I am grateful to the man. And I know John was, too.

I see this art form staying about where it is for the next few years. Personally, I see it as a way of preserving ecology, so we shouldn't get too abstract with it. We should be preserving birds as realistically as possible. But perhaps it's the nature of the artist to try different forms.

Doug Miller

"He didn't change his style, he perfected it."

I met John in September of 1972 at Point Mouille in Michigan. That was at the Midwest Decoy Contest. A carver named Jim Foote introduced us. I had just started collecting decoys, and he told me to try and get a bird from John at any cost. John told me that he had a fellow who was collecting his work and that everything was sold. And he had several other people waiting for pieces. We talked and seemed to hit it off from the very beginning. He had a drake golden-eye at the competition that finished second, and I asked him if I could purchase it. I wasn't collecting second-place birds, only first-place ones. I did that for a number of reasons, the first of which is that carvings at the time were judged by other good carvers, people like Harold Haertel, Bill Schultz, Jim Foote, sometimes Larry Hayden and John Scheeler. I thought they knew a lot more about decoys than I did, and I respected their decisions. I thought this approach made sense because all the decoys looked good to me. The only show I had been to before the one at Point Mouille was the International Show held in Davenport, Iowa. I picked up a few birds there and was bitten by the decoy bug.

I had been exposed to a lot of older birds and their designs, but the undercurrent among collectors was that there was so much counterfeiting and restoring, it was hard to discern genuine birds from bogus ones. I felt that was too risky for me. If I could have a carver hand me his bird or make me something on commission, I would feel more comfortable.

I also visualized birds going from plain and smooth into more articulated forms. The reason I felt that way is that I talked to carvers, and several indicated that if they could carve full time, they could do better, more interesting birds. Knowing they had a ready market, they could work up unusual attitudes or techniques or even unusual species. With a guaranteed buyer they wouldn't be worrying about lost time and the lengthy process involved in creating a piece of art. That's where I entered into this. I told them to do the best they could and, when finished, tell me what the piece was worth. This approach was refreshing to some because for most there were plateaus of prices. Knowing that, they measured out their time, though with competition birds, they put in a little more time, I believe. Their peers were evaluating the work and there was more scrutiny of a competition bird.

After a while I developed preferences and tastes and did some judging myself. I really felt bird carving could go further. I liked the way decorative carvers put legs on the birds and outstretched the wings. But a point was reached where I think the decoys got too decorative. I like the decoys before 1975. I like the transition period from pure folk art and the gunning purpose of the decoy to the decorative art form. During that time there was so much individual style. Carvers hadn't achieved the absolute look alike or the counterfeit bird. There was still character in the work. I enjoyed going into a room or area where decoys were being assembled for judging and being able to pick out the carvers. I recognized the style and admired them. Today, birds are so perfect, it's difficult for me to identify the maker. They're all so true to life.

Scheeler was one to keep an enduring style. He didn't change his style, he perfected it. He gave an impressionistic appearance to his

Douglas Miller, owner of the Wildlife World Museum, says that a favorite Scheeler piece of his is a Harris' hawk and rabbit. In the collection of the Wildlife World Museum.

Scheeler said he was particularly pleased with the rabbit.

work. He could paint coarsely but with depth and projection. That's what made him outstanding in his work. Still, I couldn't say who the best is. History is fickle. We know that from painters, Van Gogh being a classic example of a once-rejected artist.

John is much admired, probably the most admired among fellow carvers. He worked hard, and his relationship with me was good in that he had absolute freedom. I never told him what I wanted him to create.

We talked very seldom, and he went at his own pace. He would call from time to time and tell me what he was thinking about doing. I would tell him I loved the idea. Everything he wanted to do was a good idea, and he spent a lot of time thinking about each one. He was an amazing man, considering what came out of his mind and his hands. Yet he was a regular guy.

Judging by his appearance, he could have been a bayman, he was so rugged looking. The years showed, and time had taken its toll on his appearance. But what came out of the man was such a blessing. He surprised me, for when I first met him, he didn't seem like any kind of giant. He was quiet and humble and he kept to himself.

When I approached him about carving full time, I didn't want to be in the position of nagging him for work. I wanted something free flowing. Bill Koelpin was the first to approach me about working for me. He was a fire inspector at the time. We embarked on that arrangement, and it was very healthy for him. He set himself up and was very successful. The way it worked with John was that I took a contract similar to the one I had with Koelpin and presented it to him. I asked him if he wanted an attorney to check it over. He asked if the contract was okay with me, and I said yes, so he agreed to sign it. He didn't even read it, though he had seen Koelpin's. That was in late 1972, and the contract went on for two years, but our relation continued for eleven years. We didn't talk about contracts again.

It got to a point where he wondered what his work was worth, and I didn't want to sell any of it. So he had to make another arrangement in order that some of his work could be sold and he could be satisfied with what his work was worth on the market. Today his pieces will be worth a lot more, owing to supply and demand.

His Harris' hawk and rabbit composition is a favorite of mine. I was extremely disappointed for him that it didn't win the World Championship. His understudy won that year, but John's piece was admired by other carvers, and I think to this day that a great number of people like it. A year ago he commented to me that it was his favorite piece.

Interestingly, he was criticized in the early 1970s for having what looked like hawk eyes on his duck decoys. One particular redhead duck had a piercing predatory appearance, and people kidded him about it. He didn't make many decoys after that. He concentrated on things he enjoyed, birds of prey, for example. I did suggest that he do decoys if he wanted to get away from those monumental pieces he was working on. Bill Schultz did that from time to time.

I wish John could have seen how much reverence there is today toward his work. I think that would have fed him, knowing how he liked going to competitions and meeting other carvers. Those shows seemed to rejuvenate him, and he did win seven World Championships.

Andy Andrews

"John would take a piece of wood and start drawing on it and come out with a great piece of art."

My involvement in wildlife art and art in general really started when I was five or six years old. My father took me out to hunt, and I fell in love with hunting and birds. Ever since then I've hunted, raised, and watched birds. Several years ago I got involved in having birds mounted, ones I had shot, usually the male and female of a particular species. Once I had accumulated most of the gamebirds indigenous to North America, I started hunting in other areas of the world. I found I could hunt gamebirds twelve months out of the year. After a few years I ran out of things to go after. In the middle of that period, I began to raise upland gamebirds and waterfowl in an aviary I built in my backyard. I continued that as a hobby for thirteen years, until it became too much of a chore owing to the extensive travel that is necessary in my business.

The first wildlife art show I attended was the Easton Waterfowl Festival. For several years I had gone to Maryland to hunt, and I happened to be there when the festival was scheduled. I was impressed with the various bird carvings I saw and soon started to collect the inexpensive ones. At first they were only flat-bottomed ducks and geese. Eventually I gravitated toward the more expensive carvings simply because they were more realistic and finer sculptures—and they are still what I like.

Sometime during this period, I decided to invest in art both personally and for my company, Camshaft Machine Company. Shortly thereafter, my wife and I opened a wildlife art gallery in Fort Myers, Florida. We named it the Wild Wings Decoy Den. That's the sequence of how I got into wildlife art.

My favorite art form has always been bird carvings, and I have accumulated 300 to 400 of them. After the Easton Waterfowl Festival, I started going to the Ward Foundation World Championships. I knew of John Scheeler, but I had never met him. One day a friend called and asked me if I wanted to meet John, and would I be interested in his working for me full time. We talked about that on several occasions. I finally decided John could help me with the gallery and my investments in wildlife art. I also thought I could learn more about bird art from him than from anyone else. Everyone in the art field knew of John Scheeler, but only a couple of people had any of his pieces. Doug Miller had the vast majority of his work. Eventually I spoke to John on the phone, we came to an agreement, and I sent him a five-year contract, which he signed. We were in business. We agreed we would start May 1, 1983, a couple of weeks after the World Championship.

My first meeting with him was unique. I called his house and asked if he and his wife, Edythe, would join my wife, Sandy, and me for dinner when we arrived in Ocean City. When he agreed, I asked him when he wanted to eat dinner. He said 4:00 P.M. I thought he was kidding, but he insisted on the time. Eventually we compromised on 4:30. That was my first encounter with John, and I learned quickly that he had a mind of his own and wasn't ready to bend for me or anyone else.

Over the years, what impressed me the most about John was his honesty. He was always impressed by others who were honest, and we talked about that a lot, so I can understand why he had that characteristic. He rarely criticized a piece or a person. He did everything in a positive way. He was a very quiet and unassuming person. After I got to know him, he did come out of his shell, and when I asked him about a piece I wanted to buy, he would tell me the good things but stay away from the negative. It took two to three years before I could get him to criticize a piece of art, and then it would be only to me.

To carvers he was totally unselfish, generous, and free with advice. He had an uncanny way of critiquing another sculpture objectively and in a positive manner. I was always impressed with the way he did that.

I used to be very impetuous when buying wildlife art. John would suggest that I think longer about buying a piece, which to him meant walking away from it for a while. When I told him that I might lose the bird, he would say, "So what? There will be more." He would even walk around with me and ask what I liked or didn't like about a piece. Then, almost uncharacteristically, he would point out whatever flaws of anatomy or creativity there were. He always told me that I had better like what I bought because I would have to live with it for a long time if no one else would buy it from me. I have some pieces now that I wish I could sell for even what I paid for them.

I was with John many times when people would classify him as an innovator, a champion, a grand master, or a great artist. But he seemed uncomfortable with that. He would shuffle back and forth, but there was a quiet confidence about him. There was almost a reverence toward him when he was around his peers. No one seemed to disagree with him once he made up his mind. I always thought that was remarkable.

John wasn't always right, but people were afraid to tell him that, although he remained humble. People in his position, be they artists or successful businesspeople, usually let you know about it. He always told me he let his work speak for him.

I used to tell him he was the best, but he would say he did not

Andy Andrews also employed Scheeler. One of his favorite pieces is a prairie falcon on a rock. Andrews likes it for its "balance and serenity." In the collection of Andy and Sandy Andrews.

know about that, though he would acknowledge winning more World Championships, Best in Shows, and first-place ribbons than anyone else. He won 35 to 40 Best in Shows and an additional 125 to 140 first-place ribbons. Yet he also admitted to me that he won certain competitions because he was John Scheeler. Judges were afraid to vote against him. One time in particular he beat a friend of his, Eldridge Arnold, at The World, and John went to Eldridge and said his piece was better.

It was Eldridge, incidentally, who said to me when John died that he did not want to go to any more competitions because he often went just to have John judge his birds and tell him what he thought.

He really got me hung up on anatomy when I first got to know him. I know what ducks are supposed to look like because I had hunted and raised them, but John had the ability to look at something and immediately know what was going on. Right until the time he died, he spoke about the all-importance of anatomy. Yet he supported artists who deviated slightly from anatomical accuracy for the sake of art. I thought that was interesting.

Another thing that amazed me was that carvers like Larry Barth would mock up a model of what they planned on doing. But John would take a piece of wood and start drawing on it and come out with a great piece of art. I'm really surprised that he didn't make more mistakes. The last few months of his life, however, he did begin doing mock-ups in clay at Barth's suggestion and was excited about the prospect of becoming more productive in his output because of this.

John was known best for his aggressive birds of prey, particularly those just completing the kill. The one I like best is his goshawk mantling over a crow. John got me to like birds of prey, which are my favorite birds now. But when he started working for me, he did everything but raptors, probably because he had done so many. Then he realized how much I liked them and did a few in the last two or three years. In the beginning, however, I wouldn't tell him what to do because I wanted him to create whatever motivated him.

His last prairie falcon is one of my favorites. I like it for its balance and serenity. I now own all the pieces he did for me except a Louisiana heron and a goshawk. The latter was his least favorite because it isn't balanced. He often said that a piece of art cannot be successful unless it is balanced.

I am also very fond of his broad-winged hawk, which is hunched over in a threatening posture, as well as a merlin he did. Many people have told me that of the birds he did while working for me the merlin was his best. It is just a hawk sitting on a branch, yet it has a great deal of class.

Sandy's favorite piece is John's 1980 gyrfalcon, and she wanted John to do a white-phase gyrfalcon. He argued that she should have a dark-phase bird. Eventually we learned why. He had a dark-phase skin in his freezer. Sadly, he never got a chance to do it.

The piece that for me best creates a feeling of movement is his pair of ruffed grouse. That was the 1980 Best-in-World composition. They actually seem to be moving.

I think John innovated many things, including the presentation of birds. He didn't want habitat and dioramas to overcome the bird or prey. That is why there is power, flow, and serenity in his pieces.

John contributed something else to the art of bird carving. Many carvers have said that since his death the grapevine is dead. He kept the carving world communicating. Since then, no one seems to know what's going on.

I never knew what he spent on phone calls, but his wife told me it was a lot. John told me he couldn't stand not knowing what other carvers were doing. And he loved telling his peers what the competition was up to and needling them about that.

John will be considered in a class by himself for his sculpture, his unselfishness, his generosity with tools and techniques, and the positive way in which he critiqued wildfowl art. And I will remember him above all else as my mentor and close friend. I consider myself fortunate to have known and worked with John Scheeler.

Gary Yoder

"If he liked something you did, he came around and told you."

Part of the problem I had when I started carving was being in the mountains of western Maryland. There were no other bird carvers around. What got me interested in bird carving was Wendell Gilley's *The Art of Bird Carving*. It was about the only book on decorative bird carving at the time. That was really the start. Only after several years did I manage to find out that others were doing this.

The biggest boost came when I went to Salisbury in 1973. That's when I got my first inkling of what could be done with a block of wood and the shape of a bird. I remember being floored by the work that was there. The one piece that stands out stronger in my memory than any other is John's peregrine falcon with a green-winged teal. That was a world championship piece. I knew I wanted to carve birds like that. The piece had that kind of punch and power.

When you look at those birds now, you see that they are not as well rendered as the work done today. They are not as exact, not quite as polished, but they still have that Scheeler touch.

I can't point out what it is about a particular style that makes a person's work unique. But with a John Scheeler bird, you walk into a room and you know it's his carving. His work was one of the biggest early influences on my carving and still is a big influence to this day.

When I started going to shows in the early 1970s, I was just a kid. I was not the type of person to just introduce myself to people or start a conversation. So it was a good number of years after that first show that I got to meet John. I don't remember how or when we met, but John was always at the shows. He was a legend even back then. I was in awe of him. It was only in the last couple of years that I got to know him personally. He was a man of few words, so it was difficult to find out what he was really like. I actually learned about him through other carvers and through his carvings, which spoke volumes about him.

One of the first things that struck me about his work was the power of the pieces. John did quite a few types of carvings. But the ones that always stuck with me were his birds of prey. Those were the pieces that represented him as much as anything else.

I should point out that other carvers had styles. Bill Schultz's work, for example, was like music. Everything was composed, balanced. There was a harmony. But John's work was pure power. His birds of prey exuded that feeling. A good example was his goshawk and dead crow. Everything tied together beautifully: concept, design, a statement of power. These are the things that made his work unique.

John also had a boldness about his work, especially through his painting. To me he did some of the finest painting on a bird that you will ever see. It was not tight, detailed painting. The oil paints he used worked well with his bold style. He could do in one brush stroke what would take me ten to fifteen strokes before I could get the colors and effects I wanted.

A good example of this was on his Louisiana heron. He got a beautiful blend of carving, texturing and painting. It was one of the quietest pieces he had done, but texturally it was astounding. He had a full range from burned to stoned to smooth areas, so smooth the

Gary Yoder, who early on was influenced by Scheeler's work, says that Scheeler made a statement of power with his predator–prey compositions. He particularly likes a sharp-shinned hawk and starling Scheeler did in the 1980s. In the collection of Andy and Sandy Andrews.

A detail of the mantling wing of the sharp-shinned hawk.

effect was almost a throwback to the decoy days. He had paint on so thick he could actually texture it with a brush. He was blending old and new ideas in a carving.

He was never quite satisfied using the same techniques for piece after piece. He was working new frontiers in textural diversity, painting, and carving style. This openness is what made him so diverse.

But there was another side to his diversity. John could successfully carve a hawk or a shorebird. He could switch gears, but the bird still said Scheeler. He could get the motion and grace in a shorebird and turn around and get the power in a raptor.

Yoder says a composition like this one is a story of domination and submission. He particularly likes the way Scheeler planted one foot of the raptor on the prey.

Two of my favorite pieces are his sharp-shinned hawk and starling composition and the goshawk and crow, although the latter pair was taken a step beyond. Both compositions had the prey on their backs. This is a total picture of submission. And it is domination to have one of the raptor's feet planted on the prey in each piece. Back in 1976 I did a peregrine falcon with a green-winged teal that was not unlike John's 1973 composition. But I did not plant the foot on the prey. When I saw the way John had planted a foot on the dead bird, the design made perfect sense. Obviously, the falcon will do that, but this was more than making a statement about the falcon. This was talking about the possession, the reduction of the prey to a possession. Also, by turning a dead bird upside down and exposing the breast and soft underbelly, John contributed to that statement of submission and domination.

With both pieces everything was working in a circular motion, such as the way the wings of the hawks mantled over the birds. Even the colors of the birds worked well together.

John did a merlin on a pine branch that I liked. That was a different side of his bird-of-prey style. He did beautiful raptors without prey. Viewing his noble looking gyrfalcon on a rock is like looking at a monument. He had this pinnacle and the bird is sitting on top of it, making the composition almost a triangular piece of rock and bird. It is more a piece of sculpture than a carving.

With the more sculptural pieces done today, you can see John's influence. These are pieces that have removed the unnecessary elements from the composition, such as mud, rocks, leaves. John incorporated only elements that were necessary. He did not burden the piece. He made the bird a sculptural form.

This approach could be seen even in his pair of flying grouse. I had never seen John do grouse, so it was not typical of what I knew of his earlier work. To me it was a more stylized piece. He wasn't one to get overly picky with techniques, measuring every tiny feather. He had the ability to strip away the unnecessary elements. I'm trying to do that now with my own carvings, attempting to get the feeling across with a strong, tight composition.

I think the strongest aspect of the piece is the flurry of motion in it. The wings are in strong positions with lots of bends to the feathers, a lot of air spaces between them. Also, it is a busy piece. Leaves are flying everywhere. But as you look at the piece, you suddenly realize that all that is holding the grouse up are leaves. The birds seem to be skittering across the ground. When a grouse comes up from the forest floor, things seem to fly everywhere. That's what John was trying to get across with the birds. And he had both going in different directions. But that contributed to his composition. By having the birds go in different directions and the flurry of leaves, he managed to tell the story of flight and escape. A lot of his work had a dramatic story behind it.

John was a prime mover in bird carving. When you speak to today's carvers, such as Bob Guge, Larry Barth, Pat Godin, Jett Brunet, and others, and ask who the major influence was, Scheeler is going to be right up there.

But he was more than an inspiration. If he liked something you did, he came around and told you. That meant more to carvers than anything else. In fact, if your bird didn't get a ribbon but John liked it, that was probably more important.

In 1986 I had a quail at the shows. He seemed to like it a lot, though there were things he didn't like about it. He told me and I was glad for that kind of criticism, which is very constructive. That is a nice memory. It was also the last time I spoke to John.

Kenneth Basile

"He had a reason for the placement of every feather and rock."

I got involved in bird carving in 1974; my background had been in art and museum work. At the time I was putting together an exhibition of Chesapeake Bay decoys, a permanent exhibition at the Chesapeake Bay Maritime Museum. It was Dr. Harry Walsh's collection that the museum installed, Dr. Walsh being the author of *The Outlaw Gunner.* He turned his decoy collection over to the museum. During the installation I was working closely with Robert Richardson, author of *The Chesapeake Bay Decoy,* trying to figure out who made what decoy. I figured I might as well go to someone who knew something about decoys. I thought a decoy was just a carved duck; they all looked the same. Richardson taught me a lot about decoy identification and to appreciate the art form.

In 1977 I was hired by the Ward Foundation. I had that experience of working with decoys together with my academic background, so I was a logical choice for the job. I worked for the Ward Foundation until 1985. It was at that time that I got to know John Scheeler and got deeply involved in the bird art movement. Over the years I put together in my own mind a considerable amount of information concerning the nature of bird carving.

John Scheeler was a product of wildfowl art contests and exhibits. The art form of decorative bird carving has developed around a tradition of large community carving exhibitions and competitions. Without these vehicles John Scheeler and many other major bird carvers would never have had the exposure and inspiration to continue with their work. The activities provided them with a forum in which to evaluate, discuss, and critique their work.

The down side of these exhibits, particularly for a highly successful bird artist, is that they also attract those with mediocre skills. You can't nurture the truly talented artist without giving an opportunity to the less talented. But this is the way the art form has traditionally developed. I do think the really talented bird artists will be moving with greater frequency away from these forums.

This defection is critical to the development and future of bird art. More of these artists will be going in other directions. This will enable them to devote more of their time and energies to the process of making art.

John used to talk about the trend a lot, as do so many other bird sculptors. These people are sculptors who happen to be working with wood and happen to be working with birds as a means of communicating how they see the world. So many things play a role in how a person's vision is affected. The more creative the artists are, the more they will shy away from structured environments.

I don't think this is unique to bird carving. It happens periodically when you have a certain structure that has developed around an art form. Those who have the talent and the vision at times have trouble dealing with the structure. John saw this happening.

John Scheeler's success was largely due to Douglas Miller, who acted as his patron, and the Ward Foundation, which encouraged him

While he was museum director for the Ward Foundation, Kenneth Basile knew Scheeler. Basile says that Scheeler made his prairie falcon and mourning dove with the notion that something flying overhead distracted the raptor. In the collection of the Wildlife World Museum.

A peregrine falcon and green-winged teal done in 1973. Domination is achieved through height, not mantling. In the collection of the Wildlife World Museum.

and gave John a forum in which to display his work. They gave him an environment to work in, to display his natural talent. John would have liked to have had his work out in public more, but he at least had Miller's Wildlife World Museum and the North American Wildfowl Art Museum in which to display his work.

When John and I spoke, we talked about ideas and art more than specific carvings. We spoke about various physical and visual relationships, such as how birds fit into a space, how the eye moves over a piece, and how a composition causes a reaction psychologically and visually.

John was very aware of what he wanted to achieve when he created one of his sculptures. He was a slow worker. But I believe this was because he was so aware of what he was doing with his compositions. When John Scheeler made a piece, he had a reason for the placement of every feather and rock. Even the way he painted a bird was well thought out beforehand. He was dealing with complex visual relationships, both in the environments he created and the birds themselves. Few have been able to do anything like that.

The composition and placement of his birds appear to have been of primary importance to him. A good example would be his prairie falcon and dove with cactus. Steve Graham, now the director of the Detroit Zoo, said that a hawk would never look up with captured prey unless something was coming down on it. Knowing that, you have to wonder what John was up to. If the hawk is looking up, it has to be looking at something moving very fast. Otherwise, it would fly away. There was a lot of action going on in that piece.

He would work on these compositional ideas through a number of pieces. A follow-through is the goshawk and crow. This time the hawk is hissing or chirping with this dead crow under it. Here again was action in an instant of time. His Harris' hawk and rabbit and the white gyrfalcon and oldsquaw are visual explorations along the same lines.

He spent almost two years working on his pair of ruffed grouse, not necessarily in fabrication but in thinking about it as much as anything else. That's probably the biggest part of the creative process. These birds have been alerted to something. They're leaving town, so to speak.

He created a pair of doves on a block of wood, making a base similar to one made by Eldridge Arnold. It's a beautiful piece, soft and gentle. Looking at his paint work on a composition like that, you realize how impressionistic his use of paint was. If he had lived, I believe he would have continued working with doves and their organization and story.

John was a leader in the field because of the way he worked and saw the world. Very few people have come close to what he did. And that comes back to my overall impression of what is happening to the art form. You have maybe a handful of people who are leaders in this area of art. John was right up there. It was for many others to catch up to what he was saying and doing. He kept in close touch with a number of bird carvers. There were ideas flowing between these people. And that I find very interesting. The same phenomenon happened earlier between bird carvers. People like the Ward brothers and Arnold Melbye and Shang Wheeler shared ideas with others. I know that the same thing was and is occurring among the top bird carvers, among the idea makers. John was an idea man, collecting and bringing ideas together.

Granted, there are some bird carvers functioning at the same level as John Scheeler, but I don't see many producing the magical things he did. There will be more showing up.

I don't know where the art form was leading him visually or creatively. It would be difficult even to try to guess. But I do know that he saw some of the things I see occurring in the movement.

To be a true pathfinder, to produce images that are unique and deal with visual concepts that are of a changing nature and show different aspects of the world to the viewer, is very rare. Today there is the issue of realism and super realism. Where will bird carving go in the future? Audubon or even the Ward brothers would never make it in today's bird contests because of the stylized nature of their work. But what they created was of immense and lasting importance. We can all be sure that the one constant in the future will be change. All of us will be seeing bird sculpture that uses the bird in different ways. John Scheeler was an artist who developed a style that was uniquely his. He was free enough and open enough and secure enough to show people his visions, rather than copying the work of others. As with John, we should be seeing more and more people concerned with concepts rather than reproductions. The bird and the wood that John worked with were just the vehicle he used to express his vision and ideas of the world around him.

Robert Phinney

"He said the shows should be opened up."

John Scheeler was displaying his goshawk and crow at the 1981 World Championship. After many years of phone conversations with John, I tried to imagine what he looked like. While walking around the displays and reading the labels, I found him seated next to his wife. I saw a quiet, unassuming man.

What we talked about was his goshawk and crow. He did not like the sheen on the hawk, and he wasn't satisfied with the iridescence on the crow. He even pointed out that he had not finished the wings' underfeathers on the goshawk. In that conversation I began to see John's open-mindedness, a sense of wonder, and a lack of ego. His mind constantly scanned the horizon. It enabled him to look beyond the skills that had been achieved in bird carving and know that the field could go further.

The strength of any artist is to stay humble and not lose his sense of wonder. Certainly John had that strength. And Larry Barth rein-

Robert Phinney, noted for his bronzes of bird sculptures, talked at length with Scheeler about simpler forms. Phinney believes that Scheeler was particularly conscious of simplifying when he did his surf scoters. In the collection of the Wildlife World Museum.

forces that same notion. Larry says that he really goes to the World Show to look at the novice table. There the carvers do things that they haven't been told they can't do. They come with exciting, novel ideas and that sense of wonder.

I fully realized what Larry was talking about when I went to the 1987 World Championship. I saw a piece that wasn't given a prize. I'm not sure the person who did it really understood what he had done. But I was so excited about it, I found out who the artist was and actually asked a third party whether the artist understood what was there. I described to him the abstractness involved and why the piece was so dynamic. He assured me that the carver didn't do it intentionally.

I am going to take what I saw in that piece and make a small fortune on a series of bronzes. What I will do will not be plagiarism. I am going to add to what was begun. Whoever did it had enough sense of wonder to suggest a fine composition, but there was not enough technique for him to know how to make it obvious to everyone else.

This is why John wanted to bring outside perspectives into the shows. He said the shows should be opened up and that they should stop imposing those binding rules on carvings so that the talents that

Scheeler gave each bird an alert look. Such a piece would project as well in bronze as it does in wood and paint.

exist can do more adventurous things and discover a broader art potential.

I don't think the people doing this art form really know who they are or what they can do or where they stand in relationship to the rest of the art world. John certainly wanted to find out. But many are afraid of a loss of innocence once they do. If they retain John Scheeler's humility and open-mindedness and sense of wonder, they will have a very powerful art form. The danger, of course, is that with recognition the artist will develop a big ego and a closed mind, and then he's dead on his feet. The public moves on, and he doesn't know what happened.

I don't know exactly what effect I had on him, but I had been preaching simpler forms when we met. Since most of my work is in bronze, I would explain to him how costly every detail is and how extraneous things have to be thrown out. Anything that isn't absolutely meaningful to the whole piece is a lot of wasted energy. I've had to censor and edit portions of compositions.

In some of our last conversations, we got into discussions of abstract pieces, doing more with less, getting away from elaborate bases, loosening up the form.

What excited him in our last talk was a pair of doves he had done in clay. I believe Larry Barth had persuaded him to do clay models. They were examples of the evolution that saw him develop the abstract with underlying forms. He worked the clay with enthusiasm because it was so fast, so responsive. He could get those doves out of his head and into the clay a lot faster than into wood. Corrections were so easy. He was probably as happy with them as he would have been with the finished carvings.

He was interested in why I went from painted wood carvings into bronzes. I felt the challenge was in the form. I was always telling John to try bronze, and I offered to have his doves cast. We also thought about John, Larry Barth, and myself having a show in Manhattan. For if a person can be exposed to a broader range of viewpoints, and there are many in a place like New York, where people are super critical, then a lot of growth can be stimulated. Such a show would have been a real challenge for John, but one he could have taken on.

Larry Barth

"I can't tell you how much I value the communication we had. We understood each other."

The first show I ever attended was the fall show in 1975, in Salisbury, Maryland. My family and I had been through Salisbury the previous spring and had seen posters for a bird carving show. At that point I had been carving for several years, but it was purely on my own. It was putting my interest in birds and carving together. I didn't realize that other people were doing it, though I was aware of decoys. I had seen porcelain birds in department stores, and those had gotten me excited. I certainly couldn't do porcelain on my own as a fourteen-year-old, but I did have my dad's woodshop, and I started making birds out of wood.

Like any other carver, I was just floored by what I saw in Salisbury. There are a few pieces that I vividly recall from that exhibition.

One was a pair of black ducks by Oliver Lawson of Crisfield, Maryland. Another one was John Scheeler's prairie falcon over a dove. He had won World Class with that one in 1975, and it was in the fall exhibit. I was so impressed with that composition. I remember thinking, my goodness, here are people actually carving cactus spines. That seemed like a good example of the extremes to which people were carrying things.

The prairie falcon itself had such a look, a personality. It didn't shout out to you that it was made out of wood, as many carvings do. The man who had done it was using wood, but that wasn't obvious in the final product. The piece was birds, not wood. I was very impressed. That was the first piece I had ever seen of John's. I don't remember if I saw John himself there. If I did, I was much too timid to talk to him.

The following spring I entered in the novice class. That would have been the spring that John won with his long-eared owl and mouse. Again, I was very impressed with the piece. There was featheriness and softness about it. He could put that in a carving better than anyone else. And again, I don't remember if I saw John there. If I had, it would have been totally inappropriate for anyone so low on the totem pole to talk to the man who was the master.

The following year, 1977, was the first year I entered the professional class. I had a piece in the miniature division. It was a red-tailed hawk in flight. I was proud of that bird, and maybe that gave me the confidence to approach John. I introduced myself to him and we shook hands. I told him how much I enjoyed his work. He asked me if I was a carver and if I had anything at the show. I answered yes, and he asked to look at it. I hadn't expected that. But that was typical of John.

He looked at the hawk. It was half size, and the wings were carved out of solid blocks of wood, which has always been my style. He looked at those wings, and with a kind of nod over his shoulder at the World-Class table, he said I ought to be over there. That was very high praise.

Two years later, in 1979, I had my family of great horned owls in World Class. He came over when I set it up and introduced himself to me and started to tell me that I really had something there. I don't know whether he remembered our previous meeting. But I told him how important his encouragement had been to me.

After that, I started to get calls from him. The first time he called, I was out. My wife said I would never guess who had called. She was right. I couldn't imagine what he had wanted to talk about. He told her to tell me that one of my carving buddies had called. What an understatement.

Eventually he phoned again. He just called to chat and find out what I was working on. That's how most of our calls went.

I tried to hold up my end of the conversation, and he kept me posted on what other carvers were doing. I remember the year I was doing a meadowlark and pheasant. John called close to the show date and told me that he had been talking to Pat Godin and it sounded like Pat's piece was very similar to mine. They were alike in their basic concepts. Both were quiet pieces with a lower bird or birds and a bird up top. It scared me to death that there was going to be another composition at the competition that would be similar but bigger. John would tell you what he knew was going to scare you, and then he'd tell you that he wanted to know what other carvers were doing because it kept him sharp. He knew he was putting doubts in your mind. But he was keeping you aware that this was competitive and that you had better be doing your best. He was right.

At the same time, John Scheeler was doing something more important for bird carving. In my mind he was leading the movement away from the stereotype that bird carving had become and moving it toward bird sculpture. It's a subtle, semantic distinction. He and Eldridge Arnold of Connecticut both started to put birds on pure, geometric shapes in contrast to the busy environments that had come to be expected. John was "tired of making dirt," and Eldridge didn't feel like putting his birds in "salad" anymore. John felt the diorama approach was dated and referred to it as Victorian. He wanted the work to have a cleaner look that would be both contemporary and classic, new but timeless. So John and Eldridge started to get away from detail, detail, technique, technique. They just quit making vegetation and habitat.

At the same time John continued to work at balance. Pieces started showing up like his pair of mourning doves and his mantling kestrel. These were very clean pieces with the focus on the birds. He was working out the composition within the birds themselves.

I think the last composition of John's that had a great deal of habitat was his green heron. That piece went edge to edge with moss and plants and rocks. When he did a similar bird later, a Louisiana heron, he showed only a small amount of habitat.

It seemed that from then on his pieces took on a refined, clean look. A good example is his merlin, which is perhaps one of my favorites, where things really seem to come together. But his search for balance and simplicity can be found in earlier works. He did a gyrfalcon, for example, that was perched atop a rock, and the rock was set in dirt in a lathe-turned base. The piece is simple and straightforward and succeeds on the power and presence of the bird alone. It is interesting to compare it to the peregrine he was working on at the end of his life. In their basic formula they are the same, a large falcon perched on a rock, but there is a significant difference in the treatment of the base. Instead of being set in dirt on a turned base, John had placed the peregrine's rock in a more sculptural context by pre-

Larry Barth is considered a supreme artist in the field of decorative bird carving and was a close friend of Scheeler's. One of the first pieces he saw was a long-eared owl and dead mouse. Barth remembers that there was "a featheriness and softness" in the carving. In the collection of the North American Wildfowl Art Museum.

senting it on a clean black box. The result is less like a bird carving and more like a piece of sculpture.

John had been creating power and simplicity long before he started putting birds on black bases. The goshawk and crow composition also has a refined, clean look, and it deserves to be talked about. Though it's not fair to pin John down to a formula, he did do a lot of hawk and prey pieces. The goshawk and crow were his finest effort in that vein.

I heard more comments about that dead crow than about the live bird, the goshawk. I found the goshawk to be a whole lot more magnificent than the crow. Had I been the creator of that piece, I would have been bothered that everybody just kept on and on about the crow instead of the whole composition. You need to achieve a balance. Though the crow was a spectacular element of the composition, I didn't think it took over the piece. Both birds worked together very well.

That goshawk was such a perfect bird for John to work with. It has power and fierceness. The crow was an ideal compositional complement to the goshawk, being pure black and not fighting with the plumage of the hawk. I would have been tempted to put a grouse with the goshawk, but I don't think that John's composition would have come off nearly as well with anything other than a crow. The crow, with its solid color, allows the goshawk to take on all the color and animation. The crow allows the goshawk to be the vibrant core of the piece.

John was also after a look. He liked a fierce look, and I would say that that goshawk was as fierce as he ever got a bird to appear. I think it is one of the finest pieces he ever did, though I resist picking a favorite. To me it was his ultimate rendition of the hawk-and-prey theme he explored throughout his career.

Another piece in which balance comes into play is his Louisiana herons. They don't succeed on the basis of fierce expressions, they succeed on the working composition of anatomy. With the goshawk and crow John was dealing with mass and shape; with the herons the lines are what count. It's a linear piece. There is flow among the curves and recurves. It's a very different piece. I tend toward that kind of composition, toward quieter, gentler birds. The herons are pleasant with their balance and linear movement.

Technically, though, I got more out of the single Louisiana heron that he did later. The painting was phenomenal. John could paint like nobody else. He went beyond mixing up the right colors and putting them in the right places. John painted light and atmosphere into the plumage of his birds. The people who mattered knew this, though I sense there were some who thought he was a sloppy painter. Well, neat and tidy paint-by-number birds are easy, but few carvers can do what John could do with a brush. He was the truest painter of all of us. He wasn't just coloring his birds, he was painting them. He understood painting in its pure sense better than anybody. Warms and cools, lights, values, tones—those were words he was dealing with instead of asking whether a color was the same as that on a skin. That's one of the things I most admired. His are the only birds I've ever seen on which I wouldn't change a thing. Part of that has to do with his looser finish. Most of us are putting in every single bit of detail that we can, and when you put in everything, there's nothing left for the viewer to do but look at the piece. It becomes a one-way street with all the information going from the piece to the viewer. Everything's been done and all you have to do is look at it. John's work was looser, setting up more of a two-way street. The viewer was also able to send a little information back to it. John's approach allowed the viewer to see in the work a little bit of what he wanted along with what John wanted to show.

There was another aspect of John, and that was his restlessness. Whenever I saw him at a show, he had just been at one of the merchandizing wings and had picked up some new bit or tool. Even when he knew exactly how to do something, he was looking for another way to do it. So over the years I had built up a mental picture of his shop having shelves and cabinets with boxes and boxes of every odd and end ever conceived of, poking out everywhere, and things that he hadn't had a chance to try just lying around. But when I saw his shop after he died and found nothing there, what went through my mind was, Where was the stuff we were constantly talking about? It was just not what I had expected.

What was there was a bucket seat on a dairy case, his Gesswein on the floor. I don't know what he did with his Foredom, since you can't just lay that on the floor. There were a couple of stools covered with clay models, a small bookcase and a file cabinet, but no table space, no place to put anything. I have as much table space as I can get, and I'm still running out. Without table space, how did he stand back and look at his pieces? I can only believe that his concepts and techniques were all in his head. His shop didn't have much to it, yet all those incredible pieces came out of it. It wasn't the shop, then, that produced the work. It was John. That was the key.

Our relationship was more than just talking on the phone and at shows. We swapped materials for perhaps the last year or two. He sent me armature material for my flying terns and some Sculpey, a type of clay he introduced me to. I sent him a thrush I'd made with the Sculpey and some tools I found useful for working with clay. There is something special about having things John actually worked with in my shop. I have one bit he gave me that I know he used. I make a point to use it on every bird I do.

He stopped here once, and I didn't know he was coming. My wife came in and said that John Scheeler was in the driveway. He was on his way to Michigan. It was a brief visit, but I am so glad he stopped. I was able to show him the things I was struggling with, things we had only been able to talk about on the phone. I regret never having visited him while he was in his shop. I can't tell you how much I value the communication we had. We understood each other. A lot of things didn't have to be explained, for each of us knew that the other understood. I have as much appreciation and gratitude for John himself as I have for his work.

Floyd Scholz

"To me his birds were magical."

I've been carving birds for almost eighteen years, since 1970. I first became aware of John Scheeler as a person and an artist back in 1975, when I attended the Connecticut Audubon Society's bird carving show in Fairfield. At the time I was only seventeen years old and the exhibition was held in my hometown. There were perhaps twelve to fourteen carvers showing there. Among them were Lynn Forehand, John Garton, Jack and Betty Holt, Jim Foote, and Arnold Melbye. One carver present whose work still stands out in my mind was John Scheeler.

At the time I had never heard of Scheeler, but his birds caught my attention because they went beyond anything else at the show. He had a prairie falcon over a dove. The life he managed to portray through that sculpture remains with me to this day.

He had other birds of prey. And I stress birds of prey because few carvers were doing raptors. Even songbirds were very new. The focus was still on the waterfowl: ducks and geese, seabirds and shorebirds.

At that one meeting we spoke for a moment and shook hands. He seemed so quiet and reserved, and as a seventeen-year-old kid I

Another carver with whom Scheeler kept in close touch is Floyd Scholz. There is a great deal of intensity and balance in his raptors, says Scholz. This is Scheeler's broad-winged hawk. In the collection of Andy and Sandy Andrews.

took that to mean he was not really interested in talking to me. Looking back now, I realize that was the way he was as a person.

The following year John showed a long-eared owl with a mouse hanging from its mouth. He also had a roadrunner and a flying dove. By that time I had been carving birds for about six years. I brought a miniature wood duck along with me to show this man because I wanted to let him know that I carved birds, too, no matter how crude they seemed compared to his. It was a thrill having him look at the bird. He was not super critical and he remembered me from the previous year. I spent most of that visit standing around his table. To me his birds were magical.

John had the magic touch, even though he used the same woods and paints that others used. But John made pieces that no one else can equal. He gave his birds dignity and passion.

Looking closely at his pieces, you realize that they don't possess the technical brilliance or so-called "tightness" of some of the top artists today. John wasn't feather perfect, but he could convey something through his sculptures that very few other artists could or will be able to do. He projected the essence of a bird.

If there's one thing I learned from my association with John Scheeler, it is that it takes more than hands and eyes to produce a masterpiece. You need a soul; you need to carve with your heart.

When I spoke to him, I got the feeling that though he was doing this for a living, he was also doing it for the pure and simple love of his subject. When I heard him talk about seeing a live peregrine falcon, it sounded to me like he was talking about the first time he met his wife. He would say, "Oh, the way they look at you." I knew he had an intense love of birds.

Scholz says this pose, an upright threat, is not typical for a raptor.

We had many conversations about falcons because we shared a love of these birds. He told me one time, "You look in the eyes of a peregrine falcon and you know you've been looked at. They look right through you." I knew exactly what he meant.

After the 1976 Audubon show, our paths didn't cross again for seven years. During that time I got involved in athletics and was pursuing a career in track and field. I attended Central Connecticut State College and was in competition. I was one of the top ten decathlon athletes in the country. I was doing some carving but only in the summer, and my total output during those years in college was three or four birds. But I never lost that love of birds. I recall being in Mexico City for the Pan Am games and seeing a swallow-tailed

A view of the underside of the hawk's wing.

kite flying overhead. I just about jumped off the bus to get a better look at it.

When I traveled with the track team, I did make an effort to look at birds in different places. The end of my track and field career came with a pulled hamstring, and I thought my world was caving in. After graduating from college, I moved to Vermont in the winter of 1979–1980. What brought up my spirits, because it was a form of therapy, was my bird carving. It was then that I began to remember John's work. I was also given a Ward Foundation magazine for 1981. John's goshawk and crow had won Best in World that year. I just couldn't believe what he was doing.

In 1983 I entered my first carving competition with a crow I had done. I took it to the U.S. National Decoy Show in Melville, New York, entering it in the intermediate class. I really did not have any expectations because I had not seen what other carvers had been doing since 1976. I was just curious more than anything.

My crow won a Best in Show. But more important than that, I established a friendship with people like Eldridge Arnold. I was taken by Eldridge to meet John Scheeler, who had taken a Best in Show with a pair of surf scoters. We got talking about crows because he had admired my piece. To me it was like having God look at my work. John made some comments on the painting, the iridescent color I was able to achieve on the crow and the indigo I got using washes. I was eager to learn his secrets. I told him I was spellbound by his goshawk and crow. I asked how he got that incredible sheen on the feathers of the dead crow. They looked as if they possessed life at one time, I

A close-up of the hawk's tail.

added. I was anticipating this magical secret, but he said he bought a can of Rustoleum spray paint and did the bird with that. He didn't even prime it, he said.

It was then that I realized that the magic was in his simple solutions. Who else could have sprayed a bird with Rustoleum after spending hundreds of hours carving it?

During the competition he was very complimentary about my work. At the end he walked by and said goodbye. I told him I looked forward to seeing him at the next World Show. He told me never to lose my enthusiasm. I guess he sensed the enthusiasm I had then and still have.

I did see him at the 1983 World Show and we talked. I felt richly rewarded that I had gained a new friend.

Another of Scholz's favorite pieces is Scheeler's chukar partridge.
He says, "It looks like a bird that is in a hurry to get somewhere." In
the collection of Andy and Sandy Andrews.

I didn't see or hear from him again until 1984, when I went back to The World with a merlin and a dead wood thrush. It was my first professional entry. John said the piece was a knockout compositionally, but he made some comments about the painting. I also talked with every carver I could speak with to learn more. That was the year I had it firmly established in my mind that I wanted to carve full time.

It was in the fall of 1984 that the phone rang. I was working in the studio and somebody at the other end asked where I had been. I thought it was a prank call until I learned that it was John. I nearly dropped the phone. I was quite flattered that the master should have looked me up.

When he called, I was working on a great horned owl. We talked about the species and he said he had always wanted to do one. He told me that Larry Barth did owls and said how impressed he was with Larry's work and his contribution to bird carving. We spoke a few more times that winter. I took the great horned owl to the U.S. National Decoy Show in 1985. John had a kestrel mantled over a rock. It was a beautiful piece. When I brought in the owl, he said I had come a long way in a year.

In the final judging I placed ahead of him in the show, taking Best in Class. Winning, I told someone, was like being a soapbox racer who entered the Indy 500 and beat out Mario Andretti.

I went to the World Show that year and spent more time with John. He was showing more interest in what I was doing, especially since we were both carving birds of prey as our primary subject matter.

I began sharing with him what I saw on my excursions to the raptor center at Cornell University and a raptor rehabilitation center in Montreal. He realized that I was very involved in the observation of the living bird, that I was taking this seriously, and that I was up-and-coming. He took great interest in new artists.

We had planned to take a trip to Cornell together after he told me he was working on a peregrine falcon. I had taken a series of reference photos there that I sent with a mutual friend. He called to thank me. It was then that we planned to make the trip, which never took place.

Since we didn't see each other very often, he would send me such things as the latest catalogs on tools or paints. Before they became popular, he turned me on to Australian paints called Jo Sonja. They are acrylic-based paints, but you can work them like an alkyd or oil paint. They dry incredibly flat, and they have a fine emulsion. You can water them down and they still hold their body. Some acrylics get washed out and patchy. These are very consistent.

I don't use them exclusively, but I do use them a lot. They were developed for tole painting. Also, they have a workable life of two to three days. That means you can apply them, come back the next day, and make changes with a little water in the brush. A nice characteristic.

In 1985 I began a composition of five puffins on rocks. I spent three months researching puffins and six months carving and painting them, and they didn't do a thing at the World Show of 1986. I was ready to hang it up right then. I told John that, but he only laughed and advised me to develop the philosophy that if you win, great, and if you don't win, great. Go to a show for the joy of meeting your contemporaries and seeing what new things are being done. It's nice to win, he acknowledged, but it's good just to be a part of it. I responded that he is a seven-time World Champion and he's established. He laughed again and said not to take it too seriously.

After that, John averaged a call once or twice a week. His calls indicated that he was interested in what everyone in the bird carving field was doing. He was famous for staying in touch with all the top carvers. I think he had two reasons for doing that. One was that he was curious. But the other came from his shrewdness. If someone came up with a new technique, he wanted in on it right away. By staying in close touch with the top carvers, John would learn about something new right away. That way his work remained fresh and spontaneous, and it was certainly why his pieces could never be considered repetitive or dull.

I should point out that none of John's birds are puny or frail. He did well-fed birds, muscular and at their prime. He showed his birds at the top of their form. They are what ornithologists would call alpha birds.

One of my favorite pieces is John's goshawk and dead crow because I see it as a piece that is symbolic of his intensity, almost a self-portrait. I heard people describe the composition as violent, but I don't see it that way. I see the piece representing not only intensity but also balance. The goshawk is a marvelously adapted organism that utilizes its evolutionary tools to survive. A goshawk has to eat, and crows proliferate compared with goshawks. The goshawk is an incredibly efficient killing machine because it doesn't eat daily at bird feeders. By planting the left foot on the crow's breast and having the crow in a submissive pose, John made a statement of intensity and of balance in the food chain. It was an exciting piece because it shows the balance of nature at work. To this day, I think it remains one of his most powerful works.

In 1976 his long-eared owl was a breakthrough piece because of the subject matter and number of inserts. Prior to that I don't know of anyone who incorporated other animals into a composition with such an artistic flair.

Another Scheeler piece that excited me was his pair of preening herons. They were beautifully executed. When I asked how he planned the piece, what preliminary steps he took, he made the understatement of the year. He said he just found a piece of driftwood, carved the birds, and hoped they went together. He didn't even work them up in clay.

When he did start using clay, he told me how enthusiastic he was about the material. He said that he was working up some mourning doves with clay. He pointed out that once you get playing with clay, you don't want to touch the wood. The clay was fun. He was always understating things.

His broad-winged hawk was also a very nice piece. It was not a typical pose for a raptor. That's something else I learned from him: Be different, don't be like everyone else. I have trouble with all these carving classes nowadays because the students begin carving just like the teachers. We're losing the uniqueness of the art form, the theme variations.

John didn't teach classes, but he taught through his inventiveness. The broad-wing had a pose that a human observer would rarely see unless he had the bird cornered. The hawk would then mantle and flare up. That's known as an upright threat. That bird had a great deal of movement and balance.

Another fabulous piece is his flying chukar partridge. It looks like a bird that is in a hurry to get somewhere, and it's straining in

Scholz says that Scheeler did a convincing job with birds in flight because he understood the physics of avian flight.

flight. It doesn't look like it's hanging from a thread. It looks as though it is putting itself through the air under its own power.

Many carvers who do flying birds aren't aware of the physics of avian flight or what the muscles are doing. But this bird's body indicates the fight it is making against gravity as it strains itself. The alula feathers of the partridge show that it is entering its power stroke. Those feathers are where they should be, not flat or straight out. John certainly understood the mechanics of flight.

He understood so many other things about the birds he carved. I got commissioned in 1986 to do a life-size bald eagle. I spoke to John about it on the phone, and I told him that the client wanted it to be an aggressive bird. John said there are certain things you do to a bird to give it different attitudes. He said if you want an aggressive bird, be it a chickadee or a harpy eagle, you tuck one foot up into the breast and have the other one stepping out as if the bird is stamping its foot in protest. He did that with his goshawk and crow composition.

He also stressed the fact that each species of bird is unique. What is it about a goshawk that says goshawk and not Cooper's hawk? He

Scholz says that Scheeler looked at birds the way we look at other people to determine personalities, and he always worked to capture that personality in the bird's face. Here, the ferocious glare of a goshawk.

looked at birds the way you look at people to determine personalities. He carved his birds of prey, then, with a passion and integrity that I don't think anyone will ever equal.

There is no doubt that his birdwatching helped him. He told me he was at the Brigantine Wildlife Refuge in New Jersey one day. He saw a lot of people on this bridge, so he stopped the car and walked over. Someone had identified the bird everyone was watching as an immature Cooper's hawk. John took one look and said it was an immature peregrine falcon. It turned out that he was right.

I do a lot of research. I feel that if you're going to portray something accurately, you have to watch the living bird. Peregrines don't fly like woodpeckers, which don't fly like mallard ducks. They're all different, and that's what research and spending time in the field are all about. You must observe the living bird in order to portray it accurately.

Today there are so many reference books out that it's not difficult to get a bird to look at least something like its species. The real focal points, then, particularly in the next few years, will be the elements of design and composition. You are always going to have the middle-of-the-road carvers who will do a nice piece with dirt and leaves on a walnut base. Those carvers will be content so long as they make the birds look real. But the daring carvers will go a step further. Eldridge Arnold made a daring step by mounting his birds on a piece of polished marble, deemphasizing habitat and emphasizing the combination of color and composition.

Note the work done around the eyes of the prairie falcon.

I think there will also be more of a Japanese or Oriental influence on the art form, which will downplay the super realism and play up the essence of the bird. That may well be called the "less is more" philosophy. Bird carving will be getting away from feather-perfect birds and aiming at sculptures that capture the feeling or attitude of the bird. Abstract elements will also be introduced. I have some projects like that that have incorporated marble and carved roots.

Thanks to people like John, doors are being opened for others to go through. He has rewritten the book on what the limits of composition and balance are with birds. I believe, then, that he will have as big an impact now that he is no longer with us as he did when he was producing his masterpieces. I'll be more than pleased if I can have one tenth the impact he has had on this art form.

Every piece I do is influenced by John in some way or other, but in terms of philosophy rather than technique. I don't carve or paint like John. I'm striving for the intensity he achieved, and when one of my completed pieces "projects," I know I've come another step closer. I don't know where I'm going with it, but I'm on my way.

Marcus Schultz

"He knew what was essential in a good piece of work."

I started to carve a set of hunting decoys in 1976, when I was an ironworker. For a long time my dad had urged me to start carving: He would almost insist that I carve. But I found that idea curious and inconceivable. I was working in construction and saw that as who I was. So looking back, I wonder why he was so insistent. I still don't have the answer, but when I visited him, I would admire what he was working on, and it was a highlight of the visit to hunt or fish together.

Then I saw a pair of his service bluebills. They were so appealing to me and looked manageable. That was the catalyst. They were simplified, stylized, and sculpturally pleasing. Even the painting looked manageable.

He set me up with a couple of pieces of wood and I went home, deciding I would carve a dozen ring-necks to hunt with. That's how it started for me.

I met John the first time I went to the World Show. In 1979 my father persuaded me to enter a contest, though I had no intention of doing that. I fought and resisted. Reluctantly, I sent two birds out. Then I started to read my father's magazines with articles about who was doing this kind of thing. So in 1980, I went with my father to the 1980 World Show, looking for all my heroes. John was one of them.

John had entered a white gyrfalcon that year. At that time it was unquestionably one of the most successful pieces I had ever seen pictured or exhibited. Sculpturally, it wasn't highly animated, but that appealed to me and still does. I was cautious of a lot of animation and I still am. It's hard to get such a pose that will be enduring. But the stance of the white gyrfalcon was quiet and absolutely enduring. There would be no problem looking at that bird forever.

I did a standing wood duck, the first decorative bird I ever carved, and took it to The World that year. It was judged best water-fowl and took Second in Show and John took Best in Show with that gyrfalcon. At the time I was too naive to know what kind of company I was in.

It's hard to capsulize all my feelings about John. But in terms of the pieces, I found myself admiring each of John's things for different reasons. When I got to know him, I discovered that that wasn't a bad way to be looking at his compositions because he was continuously experimenting and innovating. Consequently, different aspects would be emphasized in different pieces.

With the grouse it was the animation I admired and the suspension of the birds. With his blue heron, what was so successful and what I must assume he was experimenting with were the various textural types that the bird exhibits. There are different degrees of softness, and there are hard feathers, a term I borrowed from John to mean any definitive feathers, like primaries, secondaries, tertials. And there was the more difficult demonstration of soft, hairlike plumes, which tend to merge and mix and require an entirely different interpretation.

Marc Schultz is another carver influenced by Scheeler. This gyrfalcon is the first piece of Scheeler's that he saw firsthand. He says, "The stance of the white gyrfalcon was quiet and absolutely enduring." In the collection of the Wildlife World Museum.

Yet John's pieces were successful without being worked to death. He painted and carved his pieces in a way that I would paint on canvas. That is, I would be more economical with detail and invent ways to suggest sufficient detail. I would let the viewer be satisfied that he is seeing enough detail but have it economical. Since I highly render my carvings, I turn around and have fun with the paintings and enjoy the process. I see that in some of John's pieces.

Schultz says that Scheeler learned to capture form, attitude, and balance in his compositions. He could "render the essentials and leave out the nonessentials," Schultz states. Nor did he overwork the details on the bird, adds Schultz.

I know he was concerned with and admired accurate plumage renderings, but I never thought he considered that to be the priority on his own work. Rather, the priorities for him were form, attitude, and projecting to suggest sufficient detail.

What I consider most noteworthy about his work, and about John himself, was his wisdom. This is wisdom in the sense that he knew what was essential in a good piece of work. Knowing that, he was intentionally able to leave out nonessentials. I saw John trying things that required planning, and consequently his wisdom and experience were evident. There are many things you cannot render if you've thought of them partway through the project. Instead, he obviously found a project and planned it with those goals in mind.

Several things come to mind about when we spoke. The Friday after the close of the 1986 World Championship, he called me and asked what I was working on. I don't remember what I told him, but he told me he was working on a peregrine. On his way home he got excited about doing one and started planning it. By the time he got home, he was able to work up some drawings. I remember thinking, what a terrific way to work, to get excited about something and immediately go to it and start working it out. As for myself, I have had to spend a great deal of time getting caught up on commission work.

I remember another conversation we had. He called me four times in one day. It was an incident that pleased me a great deal. He was painting his willet. He asked me what my painting medium was composed of. I went through it and we talked about it in greater detail than before. He was having some trouble with the oils, how they blended and how they adhered. He thought too much paint was going on to get the color. A couple of hours later he called back. He had gotten the components together, was mixing them up, and he wanted to achieve the ratio that I use. A little while later he called back and laughed with delight because the paints were doing what they had to do. The fourth call came, and he was delighted with how the oils were behaving with the medium they were in. The willet had some acrylic painting and some oil, but by that evening he was tickled with how the oils were behaving. For me that was a big moment, for here was a man who was without peer in his field coming to me for advice and finding things we talked about valuable.

I could not admire John any more if I had to. So I don't want to say that John was using my techniques. But he found value in something I had to offer.

In our conversations we would invariably talk about some specific piece of work as a way of making some point in the discussion. Because of his intimate knowledge of the history of carvings and his experience in evaluating them, he was able to distill all the important aspects of a carving in a very few sentences. In one sentence, in fact, he could say something very meaningful about a single piece of work. I was able to learn about the important aspects of carvings by listening to how John reacted to them.

We spoke about form and attitude and balance. These aspects I had seen in my father's birds, which were pleasing even before he started carving individual feathers. The volumes and forms were so solid and convincing. This became more apparent to me the more I began to learn about bird anatomy.

I often use the expression "good solid wildfowl shapes." You see some forms repeating in most waterfowl. You see some typical songbird shapes. Many birds will exhibit a repetition of these good solid shapes. John and my father successfully captured these forms. Sometimes they are very subtle, but they need to be there. A beginner, learning for the first time about such forms, tends to overdo them. John and my dad worked those forms with powerful but subtle handling so that the birds had their definitive shapes. The subtlety came from the wisdom.

John's and my father's pieces also show balance and the arrangement within the pieces. Those attributes and the economy of both men's work gave their carvings power and strength. It's a simple elegance that separates the men from the boys in this carving field. A lot of people are becoming accomplished at rendering plumage and handling paint, but the meaningful aspect of these carved birds becomes form, volume, and composition, which goes back to planning and experience.

When I look now at a finished piece, I look right past the finish. It is something I'm not preoccupied with, though I do it for my birds to the best of my ability. And I enjoy being experimental in some of the techniques I employ. But I have to say that it is not my top priority. I look for good solid appealing volumes and shapes. I try to determine whether the piece would look good if the carver had stopped with a smoothly finished piece. Would it look pleasing from a sculptural standpoint? If that piece is strong and has a good finish, then it will hold my attention for a long while.

Those forms are something that I always saw in John's and my father's birds. That's why in no way does a bird have to be highly animated for it to be successful. John was as aware of that as anyone, though he did flying and animated birds. But he did them in a way that did not grow tiresome. He did it for a design purpose. That was his wisdom.

Obviously, the bird carving genre is one of realism. Since that is what it is, I think we should take it to the limit instead of worrying about whether the field is fine art and arbitrarily making it more artsy. I believe the live birds are as elegant in their forms as anyone will ever see. When you become familiar with those forms and combine them with design and balance, enhancing them, you can do a realistic bird that is also a fine sculptural piece. It's fun for me with that orientation to notice things on carvings that give evidence of the carver's knowledge of the bird. Knowledge is why John could do upland birds, birds of prey, and shorebirds with equal success. When I see those subtleties, I get a thrill out of knowing that other carvers are looking for some of the same things I'm trying so hard to learn.

Robert Guge

"He was always searching for new ideas and new ways of doing things."

My father was carving decoys for hunting. He started doing decorative pieces, and through that I met other carvers, such as Harold Haertel. One day I just tried carving and stuck to it.

I first met John formally in 1983. I met him again in 1984, when my mourning doves won Best in World, Miniature. He had judged that and other work I had at the show. We hit it off very well.

I had seen his work before that. One of his birds, a favorite of mine, was a white gyrfalcon. Like everything else he did, it said what it was supposed to. I thought that's what made John's work so special. Whatever bird he did, it said, I'm that species, regardless of how tight the quality or detail was. That gyrfalcon excited me. Maybe it was the elegance of it, a big white bird standing on a rock. At the show where I saw it, it stood above everything else.

Just recently he did several birds with that pose, but back in 1980 it may have been the first one of his like it. It was a massive piece that commanded attention.

I also liked a ruddy turnstone composition he did. It was a big shoreline piece on an oval base with lots of rocks. The birds were nestled down between them. But they were incidental to the piece of shore.

He called me the day I got home from the 1984 World Show, and we talked on a regular basis after that. He was interested in how I was achieving the surfaces on my birds and how I painted. He was always searching for new ideas and new ways of doing things. And I think he liked to compare notes. He tried jelutong, the wood I use for my work, several times, using the methods I was employing, such as feather cutting with stones instead of knives and chisels. But he didn't like the jelutong.

I think John enjoyed talking to people he spent time with. But he was also a deep thinker and an experimenter. And he liked to talk about birds and watched them as much as he could.

Everything he did was an inspiration. He always had fresh ideas, and everything had a strong impact. I thought it was neat that he didn't have any formal training in this kind of work, and that he wasn't a raptor man, someone who raises and flies raptors. But he always did a fantastic job capturing the species.

In 1986 he judged my miniature puffin piece, a Best-in-World winner. There were about thirty pieces on the table. He thought it was the best quality and he liked the simplicity. I suppose he liked the way the birds were posed, since he talked about that on the phone. And John certainly did a good job of posing his birds.

We also talked about individual carving styles. I have been teaching seminars and workshops for several years, and John had a story concerning one of my students. He had been imitating my style almost perfectly. John watched him over the course of a year at a number of East Coast shows. The first time he saw the work, it looked just like mine. But over a period of time John noted that the carver was reverting to his own original style. It was interesting that he watched that progression, or maybe regression. John and I agreed that a carver will not be fulfilled until an individual style is reached.

I hope his role will remain significant. Although he did a lot of good pieces, John is still not known to a lot of people because his work is so limited in its distribution. But he will always remain in my mind and in the minds of the people who grew with him.

Jerry Barkley

"What inspired me was seeing John Scheeler's flying willet."

I got involved in bird carving after I saw an ad in the newspaper about decoys. I went to the Long Island Decoy Collector's Show and came across names of birds I had never heard of before. It was interesting to me, and I was surprised at how much antique birds went for. At the show I bought a machined bird, which I stained and etched to resemble a wood duck.

Later I heard about the U.S. National Decoy Show. I went there expecting to see more antique decoys. But instead I saw competition birds, and that blew my mind. I decided I wanted to get involved in carving and bought Bruce Burk's *Game Bird Carving* book. Eventually I found other Long Island bird carvers to learn from.

For a while I was basically a waterfowl carver, though I like to do all kinds of birds now. A kestrel I carved in 1987 was my first open-winged flying bird, something I had hesitated to carve because of the extra feathering necessary both on top and under the wings. This technique was something I just wasn't familiar with. It took a lot of time and study to develop and carve the wings in the open position.

There's something about a flying bird that is so much more realistic than something close winged and sitting on a base. The bird at rest tends to be solid looking, whereas the flying bird looks very light. There is also a lot of movement suggested by a flying bird. What inspired me was seeing John Scheeler's flying willet.

After the reactions I received from people to my red-tailed hawk with wings slightly open, I thought I wanted to do something else with wings open, maybe a bird not as large as the red-tail. The kestrel seemed natural. And I like the colors. It's an attractive bird.

The first problem with a flying bird is how to make the pattern. Scheeler had used a variety of materials to make a preliminary model. I used Plasticene clay. For the wings I used pieces of aluminum, which I stuck into the body. I was then able to develop the idea of the flying kestrel's shape. The clay didn't have to be too precise. But with it I could visualize the twists and turns of the body.

The next problem was the overall design. I decided that everything had to conform to a certain shape, similar to what the Japanese do when they work with bonsai trees. There is definitely an Oriental influence on my flying kestrel.

I also decided not to put a turned wooden base under the bird. I thought the bird would look too restricted. I found more flow without it. Larry Barth did that with a snowy owl and bonaparte's gull he did, using a sandy piece of terrain that flared out into nothingness. Nothing was in his base to distract or restrict the eye.

For the bird's support I used a ghost wood branch and a cherry burl. I carved one into the other so they would look like one piece. I wanted the shape of the bird to follow that branch.

I wanted to enter this piece into competition. What I had learned is that everything, including the bird and its support, is judged. Also, the bird has to be seen from all angles and has to be compatible with the elements on the base, be they leaves or branches, stones, moss, or mud. All this intrigued me when I was doing the piece. And these are concepts I picked up from Scheeler's compositions.

Originally I was going to mount the bird the way Scheeler mounted his willet, with one wing lightly touching the branch, using a support that ran through the wing and into the body of the kestrel.

But as I was putting the bird together, I kept one wing aside for a while. When I was ready to attach the wing to the body, I made up my mind to use another type of connection.

When a bird like this one is getting near its prey, the feet extend out. This kestrel has seen something and is coming down to pick it up. So the wings are extended and the legs are out and open. I then realized I had a claw I could use as the point of connection with the ghost wood branch.

Jerry Barkley learned a great deal from Scheeler's work by going to the competitions and exhibitions where his work could be seen. He remembers Scheeler's merlin on a pine branch and incorporated some of the ideas into one of his own compositions.

I used pieces of solid brass rod and hexagonal brass tubing to support the cantilevered bird and prevent it from rotating. I bent and inserted the solid brass into the body of the bird, let it extend down the leg and foot and into a carved branch, where it joined the main ghost wood limb. Two hexagonal tubes, one on the bird's foot and the other in the branch, telescoped into each other so that the bird could be removed. I had seen John demonstrate a similar connection

As Scheeler did for these needles, Barkley used bamboo slivers for his own.

in *How to Carve Wildfowl.* The carved branch and the kestrel were both made from tupelo for lightness and flexibility.

Philosophy as well as technique continued to dictate how I would design the piece. I painted the branch because the light reflection off the painted surface is different from that reflected off an unpainted surface. Painting the branch made its surface match that of the bird, and everything became homogeneous.

I used pine needles to give color and some mass to the piece. This, too, I learned from a carving of a merlin on a pine branch by Scheeler. My pine needles are three to a cluster. Knowing that judges who have done this kind of work would be looking for realism, I had to keep the piece as realistic as possible. That is why I checked the number of needles on pine trees in my area. At first I tried using copper for the needles, but I found copper hard to shape and insert. Also, I noticed that real needles are very straight, and I couldn't get that effect with copper. I finally used bamboo, which, I learned, Scheeler had used for his needles. They looked better than metal and glued better. I probed into the branch with a dental pick to insert each needle. On real branches needles are missing, so I cut notches for missing needles.

On the ghost wood, I even carved growth rings in places where I broke off pieces of branch for better proportion.

This kestrel composition has won me a Best in Show in professional class at the Garden State Wildfowl Carving Competition and Art Show held in New Jersey; the New England Wildlife Exposition and Competition; Second Best in Show at the Pennsylvania Wildlife Arts Festival; and a second-place ribbon at the North American Wildfowl Carving Championship in Livonia, Michigan.

There is so much to say about John's work. Every time I went to the World Competition I went to see and photograph his pieces. I regret now that I didn't get more information from him when he was alive. By knowing carvers like John, I don't have to reinvent the wheel.

Habbart Dean

"He was strong on competitions, feeling they kept him keen."

I got started in bird carving by wanting a tie tack and not being able to find what I wanted. I took a small piece of wood and cut out a duck profile and made my own tie tack. From that I started doing some primitive pieces and became so enthused, I started making decorative pieces and became involved in the Ward Foundation, now as vice-chairman. I saw all this as a great opportunity to explore a part of our culture I had not been aware of before.

I remember very vividly the first time I met John. It was at my first competition in Ocean City. He had been a judge and I asked him if he would critique a piece I had in competition. He readily agreed. He was probably the most tactful person ever to evaluate one of my birds. He never said there was anything wrong with it. He simply pointed out some areas and suggested that I try this or that technique, just doing it in a very positive manner. As I got to know him, I discovered that this was his typical approach with regard to any person or topic. He rarely spoke in a negative manner.

The first time I visited him was when I was working on my first open-winged bird. We had been talking frequently on the phone. One night I was talking with him and he asked how my skimmer was coming along. I guess he picked up something in my voice, and he asked what was wrong. I explained. He said to bring the bird up to his place. The next morning I was on the road. About fifteen minutes after I got there, he had me straightened out on the problem I had been wrestling with.

He asked why I hadn't visited him before. "Don't hesitate from now on," he said. "Don't come only when you're carving a piece." He made me feel extremely welcome. After that we spoke to each other about once a week, taking turns calling each other. John would even visit me at my home in Bishopville, Maryland, without any particular purpose, just to visit.

I think John was the greatest person to inspire contemporary carvers. He was innovative and would pass his ideas on to anyone he thought was seriously interested in carving. He was most willing to share.

He talked, for example, about feather insertions quite a bit, about bending groups of feathers. He had shown me that technique before the book featuring him came out, *How to Carve Wildfowl*. It was a great method for getting all the feathers to have a common bend. He spoke about shaping the primaries after they were painted and inserted by using a spray bottle of water to wet them, then bending them on a flat surface and taking a hair dryer to set the feathers.

He pointed out the ways in which feathers came out of the wings of birds, the positions they take, what they do, and their relationship to the next set of feathers. He was so observant when he studied a bird, whether it be a mount, a live bird, or a carving. He seemed to have the ability to see everything. I think this was only one of the things that made John so great. He could observe and retain what he saw and do the interpretation in wood.

I remember how he spoke about the dead crow he had done for his goshawk composition. He told me he had achieved the lifelessness in the crow by carving ball and socket joints, not unlike the bone structure of a real bird. When he lay the carved crow down, he could change the bird to conform to the overall composition. This is typical of what he would share with an interested carver.

I don't think there is any question that John was one of the Ward Foundation's most ardent supporters. I know that at times he was dismayed when some of the carvers would not make the trip to the exhibit at the fall show, held in Salisbury, Maryland. He would even call them. He was forever supporting the Ward Foundation, thinking it was the motivating organization for many of the carvers, that it allowed them to be recognized throughout the world for their accomplishments.

The Ward Foundation will be following one of his suggestions for 1988. The World Class Lifesize Decorative category, now named the John Scheeler Memorial Award, will not be restricted to one group of birds, such as birds of prey or songbirds. It will be open for any bird. Therefore, the best songbird will be up against the best waterfowl, which will be up against the best seabird and so on. The competition started off this way, but it changed in 1982.

I recall a conversation we had relating to competitions. He asked me whether I do the same quality bird for a commission and a competition. I said I do. He answered, "Good. You can only learn by improving on every piece that you do. A piece done for commission should be as good or better than one done for a competition." He was strong on competitions, feeling that they were something that kept him keen.

I have a number of other memories of John. One of them was at the 1986 Easton Waterfowl Festival. I had a canvasback I had not completed. One of the eyes was not quite right. As I planned to correct it, I put that side of the bird away from the aisle. John came behind the table, sat down, lighted a cigarette, and almost immediately asked what I was going to do about that eye. He didn't say something was wrong. He simply asked what I was going to do about it.

When he was doing his last bird, a peregrine, he called me and said he had had one of his greatest experiences. A falconer had paid him a visit with a live peregrine. The raptor was something to see, he said, sitting on the falconer's shoulder. He was ecstatic.

John had told me that he had an appointment with his physician, and after returning home he called me and said he was going into the hospital on Sunday for surgery. He asked me if I could come up on Friday and spend the day, which I did.

I went into his shop, where he had his unfinished peregrine. When I saw it, my first thought was that it was the live bird he had been telling me about. But John was more excited about the rock he had the peregrine on, and he told me how he had achieved the finish.

The bird was great not for any single thing. It was the overall presentation. John seemed to capture every aspect of the falcon and its natural setting. The piece was the expression of an aggressive bird sitting on a rock, just waiting to pounce into action. John was an artist who would pay attention to every little detail as to what took place in every part of the body when the bird moved. This is only one of the things that made his work so lifelike.

He had no trouble capturing the life even with birds that had their wings outstretched. A clapper rail he did was a good example. The action he was able to get into the wings with each set of feathers working separately and yet in coordination with each other was amazing. There was never just a collection of inserts stuck into a wing slot.

And there was his ability to paint. He told me of the technique he was using to paint the breast of the peregrine. He was using a bristle brush, holding it in his thumb and forefinger, dabbing at the wood.

He told me he was having trouble concentrating on that peregrine for the last couple of weeks knowing he was going to have surgery. Sometimes I think he had a premonition of what would happen. He got out some photographs of birds, and among them were chickadees on a branch. He told me to give them to Ernie Muehlmatt. I told him he would be seeing Ernie in a few weeks at one of the shows. He said, "No, you take them and give them to Ernie."

The last day I visited him, we talked about the future of competitions. He thought there would be other mediums for competitions besides wood, birds in bronze, marble, or other material. He believed that if bird carving is to take its place as an art form, it has to bring in the best artists of all mediums.

I would like to add that in memory of John, the board of trustees of the Ward Foundation voted to establish a John Scheeler Memorial Fund. This will offer a scholarship fund for youth who will perpetuate wildlife art. There will also be a suitable memorial in the North American Wildfowl Art Museum of the Ward Foundation.

Long-term, John will be seen as someone who achieved a level of interpretation far beyond anything just lifelike. His standards will be our guidelines, not just as an artist but also as a gentleman.

Ernest Muehlmatt

"If your name was written on John's door, you were one of the boys."

I think John started to carve seriously in 1969. I started about the same time. I was a florist and got into this because I was fed up with the flower business and wanted something I could enjoy doing.

I probably met John at one of the early Salisbury shows. The first one I went to was in 1969. John was probably there.

The first thing I remember about John that impressed me was his use of the Foredom tool at a time when the rest of us were using knives. By using the Foredom, he got real muscular, bumpy looking birds. They were different from what anyone else had been doing. You just can't carve muscles and bumps with a knife as well as with a Foredom.

I remember seeing a canvasback duck he did, and on it was the most gorgeous head with muscles in the cheeks and a nice sturdy neck. I guess that was the first time I talked to him at any length. He told me he had used the Foredom and explained how you make muscles and bumps with these different cutters. Then over the years I got to know him a little bit better at each show.

He was a quiet guy but fun to talk to. He had a lot of opinions on everything, a lot of good ideas as well as new ones. He came up with innovations on how to make grass and leaves and rocks, new tools to use, new combinations of paints. I don't think there was anything he didn't try. If he thought that putting a piece of wood with paint on it in a microwave oven would crackle the surface, that was fine. He helped me a lot with that kind of thing.

I did this blue jay cluster made of tupelo, and I sealed it with Krylon spray and painted it. But I lost all my burning lines. Right away I was on the phone to John to find out what I did wrong. He said that the tupelo was so spongy it sucked up all the Krylon and that I should have soaked the bird in lacquer instead. Which I did. He had an answer for everything.

With my 1987 cluster of stellar jays, I used lodgepole pine with the composition. The needles are made out of bamboo. That was a John Scheeler idea that came from a merlin he put on a pine branch. I asked him what he used for the needles. This was during our weekly talks. He had gone to K Mart and bought a garden rake. He cut the tines off and cut up the lengths with a razor blade. These he split and then ran the needles through his fingernail to give them a slight curve. That's what I did on the lodgepole pine. I don't know how else I could have achieved that same effect with another material, like metal. He also told me about using Krazy Glue and a burning pen to secure the needles. Touching the glue for a moment would set up the bond.

He was the first guy to make paper leaves out of shopping bags. He explained how he did that, and I improved on what he said. I think he burned and shaped the leaves with a burning pen before he painted. I experimented and found it was better to paint first and then burn, sealing the paper if necessary with a lacquer or Krylon.

He was probably the first guy to use Durham's Rock Hard Water Putty for making rocks. He suggested rolling a little ball of Rock Hard Putty and dropping it from about four feet onto the floor to make a pebble with cracks. He was tickled with that idea.

Another thing about John, he wouldn't mind criticizing something you did. If he didn't like something, he would tell you why and how you could do better. I thought that was invaluable. So many carvers are afraid to hurt your feelings. He even criticized his own work. He did a piece with ruddy turnstones and rocks. He was very displeased with it. He just didn't like it, and he told me so.

But he didn't feel this way about many pieces. We both liked the goshawk and crow. I thought the crow was outstanding. I also liked his merlin on the pine branch. But probably my favorite piece was his pair of mourning doves. This was a very artistic piece. The design gave the birds an S curve. This is right up my alley with my flower arranging.

I liked the last piece he did, the peregrine on a rock. It had a nice attitude about its head and face. John was good with expression. And he was good with the part you would probably see first, the chest, which had nice rolls and ripples. It looked as if you could plunge your finger right into the wood. I achieve that kind of softness with burning, but he did it with contours and paints, which is much harder to do.

John loved the telephone. He had a door to his shop with all the telephone numbers written on it. At his funeral I went into his studio. Edythe let us wander through the place. It did me a lot of good to see the door and find my name on it, though it was misspelled. If your name was written on John's door, you were one of the boys. It was like being in the *Who's Who* of bird carvers.

Maybe the telephone was a way for him to make up for not liking to demonstrate, which bothered him a lot. Years ago at Salisbury I got into a decoy competition, and we were supposed to paint scaup. I didn't know anything about scaup, but John did. We sat down to paint, and he just couldn't do it. Everyone was trying to see his painting techniques. Finally he quit. I was sitting near him and hoping to copy what he did. But he didn't like people watching him. Yet he could have gone home and painted a dynamite scaup. Later he told me he couldn't paint under pressure.

So he communicated over the phone. He was the house organ or newsletter of the bird carving world. He could tell you what everybody else was doing. In 1985, the year I entered The World with a great horned owl, he was right on top of things. He would call and say someone else was having problems putting the wings on and another carver was having problems with the feet and Larry Barth had a crack in his snowy owl piece. It was great listening to him. He'll be remembered for a long, long time.

Curtis Badger for Wildfowl Art

"A strong, silent force which will not be replaced."

The death of John Scheeler in January marked not just the passing of one of the most talented wildfowl artists working today, but it signaled the end of an era, the loss of a force and personality that solidified and personified contemporary wildfowl art.

Scheeler, a quiet, unassuming man, was the unofficial leader of the contemporary wildfowl art movement, which had its beginning in the early 1970s. He was universally respected by his peers, as both a man and as an artist. When he died at age 62 in Mays Landing, New Jersey, the world of contemporary wildfowl art lost a strong, silent force which will not soon be replaced.

"John was unofficially the leader of carvers," said current World Champion Larry Barth of Stahlstown, Pa. "He almost singlehandedly kept us in touch; he developed such a strong sense of camaraderie among artists. No other individual could do this. He was always sharing."

It is difficult to separate Scheeler the man from Scheeler the artist. The qualities that brought him admiration in one realm of his life carried over to the other. "John was the sagest person I've ever known," says Barth. "He had that kind of wisdom that somehow goes beyond having your facts lined up. He had complete understanding of the whole scene of wildfowl art. He had the ability to know what was important and significant.

"His work embodies the same qualities. He could cut through the clutter and get to the heart of things. He knew what was essential for a piece to be powerful sculpturally. He seemed to know instinctively what was important and relevant. That was his greatest influence on my work, the need to get to the heart of things, knowing that it is the foundation that mattered, not the details."

For someone whose life had enormous impact on the art form, Scheeler's career was ironically brief. He was an industrial painter for much of his life, and he did not begin carving until he was in his middle years. Still, he managed to win seven World Championships — one in Decoy Pairs, six in Decorative Lifesize — and he collected some 200 first place and best in show awards at various carving competitions around the country.

Remarkably, Scheeler did virtually no carving until he was about 43 years of age. He once said he made a rig of hunting decoys around 1950, and took art lessons for a few months as a youth, but he had no intention or desire to be a wildlife artist until 1969, when he visited the Ward Foundation's Wildfowl Carving and Art Exhibition in Salisbury.

After seeing the work on display, Scheeler vowed to come back the following fall as an exhibitor. So after nearly a year of carving and painting, he submitted samples of his work to the selection committee in the summer of 1970 — and was immediately turned down.

While some budding artists might have considered such a rejection a personal snub, Scheeler accepted it as a challenge and renewed his efforts to perfect his vision and technique. He worked tirelessly, in every spare hour, and the dividends came quickly. He won Best of Show at the U.S. Open in Babylon, New York, in 1971, and in 1972 he astounded the art world by winning both major categories of World Class competition at the Ward Foundation World Championships. His American kestrels won in Decorative Lifesize, and his red-breasted mergansers won in Decorative Decoy Pairs. With those wins, Scheeler kissed industrial painting goodbye and became a professional wildfowl artist.

In the decade that followed, Scheeler was a consistent winner, and in his unassuming way be began to exert his quiet, strong influence on the art. His subsequent wins in Decorative Lifesize came in 1973 (Peregrine with Green-winged Teal), 1975 (Prairie Falcon with Dove), 1976 (Long-eared Owl with Mouse), 1980 (Ruffed Grouse), and 1981 (Goshawk and Crow).

Scheeler's carvings are very realistic, but realism never intruded upon his artistic sense or vision. He used the reality of nature as a tool to achieve his artistic ends. "When you put a lot of modeling in a bird, you can't finish it right down to the last detail," he said. "Instead you have to create an illusion. There is a lot more to the bird than the final finish. You can't put icing on the cake until you make the cake."

"I'll remember John most as an artist, an innovator, a pioneer, and a critic," says Roger Schroeder, who was working on a book about Scheeler at the time of his death. "I first met him when I wrote *How to Carve Wildfowl*. He not only contributed to his own chapter, but he also helped me choose several of the others for the book, including Larry Barth and Larry Hayden. He later asked me to write and photograph a book about him and his work. We decided this volume would portray his carvings as more than composites of techniques and tools. It would show his birds as works of art."

Scheeler's lifestyle and working techniques were reflected in the strong, uncomplicated, three-dimensional carvings he created. "John worked in a simple studio between the laundry room and garage," says Schroeder. "Plywood sheets covered the floor and dark paneling was on the walls. Sitting in an old automobile seat, he shaped his birds, put them on black bases or pine branches or stones carved from wood, and painted them in his own unique style. No other carver will create bird compositions in quite the same way. John and his art will be missed for a very long time."

He will especially be missed by the younger generation of carvers, who often looked to Scheeler for advice on different aspects of the art world. "When I came on the wildfowl art scene he was already a Master Carver, and I was a little intimidated by him," says Larry Barth. "I was scared to go up and talk to him. But once I got to know him we became very good friends. I feel sad for the future, but I'm incredibly grateful I got to know him as well as I did. Now that he's gone, I realize that a big part of going to Ocean City (for the Ward Foundation World Championship) was the chance to put my work in front of John."

"John's legacy is more far-reaching than the outstanding works rendered by him," says artist Habbart Dean of Bishopville, Maryland, vice chairman of the Ward Foundation. "Regardless of the subject of conversation, his humanistic approach was outstanding. Whether critiquing or judging, he was the epitome of objectivity."

Dean's work, as that of many contemporary artists, has been

greatly influenced by Scheeler, and in the past year or so Dean and Scheeler talked often. Dean visited him in his studio a few days before he was admitted to the hospital in Mays Landing. "When I walked into his studio he was just finishing his peregrine pitched on a rock, a dynamic sculpture. I immediately thought of him telling me a short while ago of a falconer coming by with a peregrine and of his exhilaration in relating that experience. As I attempted to express my feelings on the piece, he was more excited about how his rock had turned out and of the paints he had used in finishing it. Later that day he went into detail about his clay model of a sharp-shinned hawk in flight, explaining that Larry Barth had encouraged him to do his pieces completely in clay before doing them in wood. Now I know why that was such an outstanding visit with John."

Dean describes Scheeler as a man of great strength and confidence, an astute observer of every facet of nature and wildlife. "He was a catalyst for all aspects of the art form. In addition, the rapport he had with artists in all media gave him a perspective that became a source of assistance to everyone."

Scheeler was devoted to his art, and to his family. Says Dean: "Frequently he would speak of his family and I was relatively certain that there was something much deeper than that which he had verbally expressed. He once told me about a grandson who 'helped' him paint a major piece after John had left the studio. That subtle smile as he told the story was equal to anyone else's hearty laughter. It seemed to convey a feeling of deep affection."

Dan Brown was one of the founders of the Ward Foundation, and he watched closely the progress of Scheeler's career. (Dan even admits serving on the exhibition committee of 1970, which rejected Scheeler's work.) He calls Scheeler an "unassuming giant" of the carving world. "Meeting him casually at an exhibit one would never dream that John was a champion both as a person and as an artist, never looking back but always looking forward to his next project.

"A leader in his profession, John was often imitated, but he never harbored trade secrets," said Brown. "He was always willing to help you with a problem you might be having with your work, and often he would volunteer some new technique he had just devised. Many times he would take from his pocket a small burr or grinder and say, 'Have you ever tried this . . . ?'

"Somewhere up in Heaven there is the sound of a whirling Foredom tool. Surely John is fashioning wooden doves for St. Peter. The Michelangelo of bird carvers will be missed."

PART THREE

Techniques

in the words of John Scheeler

I WAS BORN IN MAYS LANDING, NEW JERSEY, IN 1925. I don't know why I stay. I just like it. I did live in Vineland, New Jersey, for a while, from age nine until I went into the service. But I like it here. None of my relatives traveled much. And I could do this kind of work anywhere.

My first job was in a foundry. I was sixteen when I quit school and went to work there. I guess I worked at that place for about six months. I was putting in forty hours a week and making more than my father. That was Depression time. But the guy had to lay me off. He couldn't take out social security because I wasn't old enough.

I'd clean up castings, break up iron, car motors. I used to start in the morning and by nighttime I couldn't stand the heat. Later they used to make machine guns, throw sand over them to cool them down. Next morning we'd dig them out.

I always had an interest in birds. I checked out birds' nests with my brother, even robbed some. Then I got into hunting. In the evenings after work I'd take a ride to a wildlife refuge and watch ducks fly in. Even to this day, my eyes are more on the sky than on the road. If I take a ride somewhere, it's going to be where birds are. That's why I go to the Brigantine National Wildlife Refuge. And I carry my binoculars with me all the time.

Scheeler at work on a willet.

The First Decoys

I carved ducks early on. The first one I did was a broadbill, using a specimen. But it looked more like a black duck, so I converted it into a black duck. It wasn't long after that that I started doing decorative pieces. But I liked doing decoys. I liked to keep them simple. The nice thing about decoys is that you can pick them up, hold them. With decorative pieces you can't do that. You have wings sticking out, birds preening. You have to be more careful with them.

I did a little painting, still lifes. I took the Famous Artists course that was in Connecticut. It was a correspondence course. Some of the top illustrators out of New York City were part of it. You'd get an

Scheeler may have been the first to use a grinding tool called the Foredom for bird carving. He and others said that it made sculptors out of carvers. A large steel ball-shaped cutter can remove wood quickly, especially if the wood is a species like tupelo gum.

assignment, do it, send it up there, and they'd tear it apart. Sometimes they were really rough on you. It cost $500, a lot of money. I dropped out when one of my daughters got sick, but I wanted to learn about painting so I could make my decoys more realistic. I still have the reference books.

I heard about a show down in Salisbury, Maryland, and when I walked in the door, it nearly blew me away. I couldn't believe what I saw. So I went home and carved. I didn't know much about ducks except local ones like black ducks and mallards. I went looking for specimens and went to the shore and waited around for some hunters to come in. I asked this one guy what he had shot, and he said a bluebill. But on thinking back, I know it was really a bufflehead. So I started collecting duck specimens and tried to copy them.

I went back to Salisbury in 1970. They didn't have the competition at that time. I wanted to get into it, but they were quite fussy about who entered. I did a pair of teals. I thought they were pretty good, painted nice. But I wasn't paying much attention to anatomy. I had a bill on the drake that could have passed for a broadbill's in terms of shape. I took them down and the jurors looked them over and couldn't accept them. So I went home and did them over. I made them as accurate as I could. They finally let me in.

I had the rejected ones on the display table and this guy asked if any of them were for sale. I said they're all for sale. He said he would take all the birds. Somebody came up to me later and asked me if I knew who that was. I told him the man had introduced himself as DuPont. He said that's one of the famous DuPonts.

DuPont liked the overall effect of what I was doing. He didn't care that the birds didn't look like taxidermy work. I don't say you shouldn't keep the birds accurate. But ninety percent of the people don't know if the work is accurate. They know what they like. Still, you should make the work as accurate as you can.

When I started competing, I started out in professional class. I never entered amateur. The first year I got a Best in Show at the U.S. National Decoy Show. I try to get a piece there every year.

I doubt that I'll ever enter the World Championships again. It takes nearly six months to work up a piece for it. And the way I'm set up now, I'm under contract to do five birds a year. There's no time for a World piece.

I prefer to work for somebody rather than myself. If you're working on your own, everybody is calling you up and asking if the bird is ready. When are you going to start my bird? they ask. I don't want any part of that.

But I still like the competitions, though they can ruin your stomach. The more you win, the more people expect of you. If you slip a little bit, they wonder what's wrong with you, if your eyes are going bad or if you're sick. I think that the good carvers are competing against themselves after a while.

There are maybe twenty top carvers around who are capable of winning consistently. And there are a lot of good ones who don't compete, like Grainger McKoy, Arnold Melbye, the Reverend Drake. But the competitions are a quick way to get recognition. And they keep you sharp.

Early Tools and Techniques

There was a friend of mine who had a woodworking shop up the road, about five miles from here. There was this guy working for him who had just gotten out of prison. He was making these realistic horses out of cherry and basswood. I imagine he learned this in prison. He was using a grinding tool. I picked up a Foredom locally and carved all my birds with it. At the time everybody else was using drawknives and rasps. I told everybody I knew about the Foredom. I got one for Larry Hayden, Al Glassford, Bill Koelpin. It took off like wildfire. Everybody had it within two years.

You don't have to have a vise with it. It's a sculpting tool. Some of the old-timers were against using it. They liked the basic tools. I said so what. No buyer has ever wanted to know what I used to make a bird, whether I used a Foredom or chewed the wood. The end result is the main thing.

Texturing started on the West Coast. A carver named Roger Barton was working with files, and Julius Iski started texturing on the East Coast. Iski is the carver I picked this up from and the carver who inspired me the most. Barton was using rifflers and Iski was using gouges. Before that, everything was smooth. Soon everyone went to texturing.

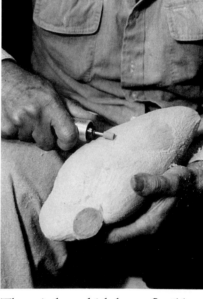

The grinder, which has a flexible shaft, can refine the wood with smaller bits. The bit seen is a Karbide Kutzall.

Above *Unfinished goshawk, 1986.* Right *Scheeler differentiated between what he called hard and soft feathers. Hard feathers have clear-cut definitions, but soft ones are lacy in appearance, as seen on the breast of this unfinished goshawk. This look is achieved with a small grinding stone.*

Then burning came in. Drake was the first one to do burning, Maggioni probably the second, and then McKoy. But it was around a few years before it got picked up by a lot of carvers.

Back then burning was done with Unger soldering irons. They were tough to use. They had different cartridges you put in for different amounts of heat. Then a guy came out with a lightbulb box that let you regulate the heat. But that didn't last too long. Colwood Electronics finally came along with a rheostat box. It's based on the same principle as the lightbulb.

Burning looks real good on feathers that are really defined, like wing coverts and primaries. But if you get into a solid color like the white on a canvasback breast, I think you're better off texturing, lacing the feathers. You can't pick out an individual feather on a solid-colored bird. On a goshawk, for example, I don't define feathers on the breast the way I would on the back. You can't see them, only groups. I'll do a whole group of feathers, making a suggestion on the edge of the group. If you did otherwise you'd end up with fish scales. That would be a hard look, whereas the feathers are really soft.

But you have to be careful what you burn. When you work a wood that has sapwood and you go across the grain lines, you get a wider burn on the sapwood than on the grain lines. You have the whole bird done, and those lines telegraph through the paint. You don't have that problem so much with basswood or tupelo.

Above *Note the chesty look of the bird, a look that was not successfully achieved before the advent of the Foredom.* Left *A profile view shows the transition between the soft breast feathers and the hard feathers on the back. Scheeler softened the look of the leg feathers with a grinding stone.*

Right *For the soft feathers on the flank of a clapper rail, Scheeler both stoned and burned in groups of feathers, a technique many carvers use to achieve depth.*
Above *A painted flank of the same clapper rail.*

Choosing Tupelo

The wood I like to use is this tupelo gum. I can get big blocks of it. I even got in the mail a piece with thirty dollars' worth of stamps on the wood.

You only use the first four feet of the tree. That's the bole. The tree grows fat at the bottom and then straightens out. There's hardly any grain at the bottom. The commercial people cut the tree up for baskets. I like it because it doesn't have the fuzziness that basswood has.

The Cajuns in Louisiana use it soaking wet. They liken it to cutting potatoes with a knife. They'll keep it wet when they're roughing out the bird, and at the end of the day they'll put it in the freezer or wrap the wood in a wet towel. Then they hollow it out, which takes the stress away from the inside and helps prevent splitting.

They'll take a chunk and sketch a duck on it and take a short hatchet and start hacking away at it. That's the way Tan Brunet and the others down there do it. Their birds are all one piece. They don't want seams. You see, you can't burn over a seam with a burning tool. It shows wherever there's glue. You'll see the line through the paint.

I like the way tupelo textures with grinding stones. You never run into the fuzziness you get in basswood. And it can be extremely light. If you want a bird in the air, you won't have to hollow it out as you would with basswood.

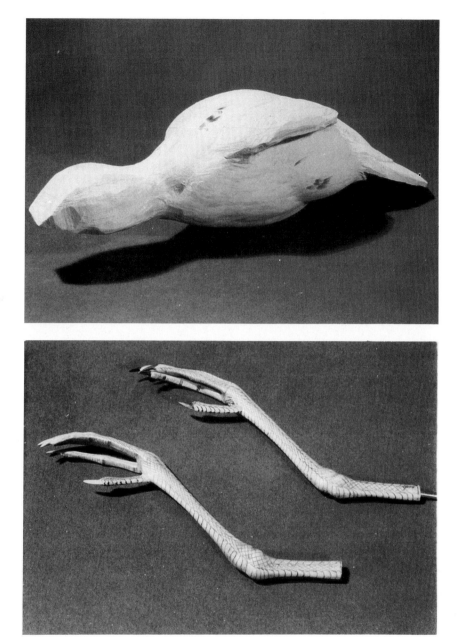

Above *For at least his last fifteen carvings, Scheeler preferred tupelo gum. Available from southern swamps, it can be cut into fairly sizable sections with little cracking as it dries out. Scheeler got this piece from Louisiana.* Above left *Because tupelo is light in weight, Scheeler was able to put birds into flight without having to hollow them out. This is the solid body of what became a flying chukar partridge.* Left *Tupelo also lends itself to extremely fine detail. Scheeler did these feet from single pieces of tupelo.*

I tried jelutong, but I don't like it. It has bad places running through it, like little slivers cut out. But you can get it super smooth.

With the tupelo I don't have to insert bills. It's a tough wood and flexible. I hear that's because the grain interlocks. When I'm finished with a bird, I'll soak the bill with Krazy Glue. It will harden the wood right up. But I don't want to put that on too soon. I may want the bill a little limber in case I hit the bill against the wood. Once you put the glue on, it gets so hard, it becomes brittle like plastic.

I can do feet, too. I make all my feet out of tupelo and burn them.

Scheeler also planned on doing a pair of doves. This is one of the doves with clay-covered metal wings.

Making Models

For the longest time I thought working up a model of something was a waste of time. But with the quality of carving being done today, you almost have to do it. Everything Larry Barth or Barton Walter does starts out in clay. They do fantastic pieces.

Some carvers say that once they do a clay bird, they lose their enthusiasm. They don't want to do the bird twice. That might be true if you're putting in a lot of details, but what I'm dealing with is form and attitude. That's the most important stage. You can be the finest painter in the world, but if the form isn't there, you have nothing.

I've seen pictures of things I wanted to do, but you don't know what's going on on the other side of the bird. With the clay you can fuss with the body until it makes sense. You have a three-dimensional pattern, I guess.

What's nice about clay is that you can make corrections in it. You can take away or add. You're actually doing your own piece, not copying. Once you're satisfied with it, it's easy to read because it's all one color. The outlines of feathers aren't going to confuse you. It's great for getting the form you want.

When I did my surf scoters, I used Plasticene and a Styrofoam armature for the body. For the tails I just used cardboard and put tape over it so it wouldn't draw the moisture out of the clay. I did the head

Above *Scheeler often did models of birds as a way of planning the pose and the attitude. Here he used Styrofoam with cardboard wings and tail for a ruffed grouse in flight.* Left *Clay also lends itself to study models. Here, Scheeler uses a modeling tool on one of two terns. Such a pose would be difficult to work from a paper pattern. For this model, aluminum was substituted for cardboard wings, and clay was easily added to the metal.*

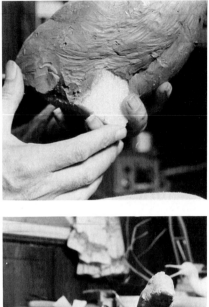

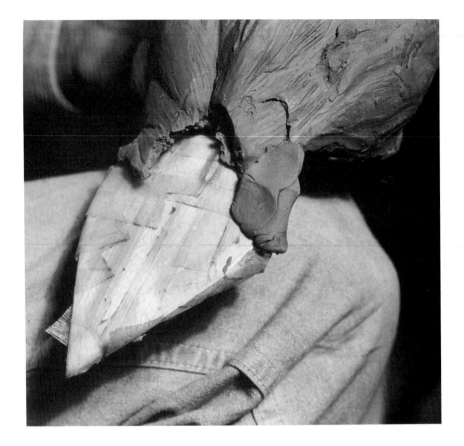

Above *A good form or pose was important to Scheeler. This is a clay and Styrofoam model of a surf scoter he did.* Top left *The Styrofoam armature protrudes through the clay.* Top right *The tail is cardboard wrapped with tape. The tape prevents moisture in the clay from being absorbed by the paper.*

of a hawk by putting wax over a piece of Styrofoam. I just wanted to see if I could do it.

If I'm doing a flying bird, like a sharp-shinned hawk I'm planning, I'll use aluminum siding for the wings and put Plasticene over that. I can cut the aluminum out with scissors.

I did this with some doves I've got in the works. I used thin aluminum and brass for the tails and put clay over that. The forms are pretty anatomically accurate. They'll be on a pine branch close together. You'll always see doves in flocks, usually in an even number. They mate up and pair for life.

With clay I feel I can put a bird in any position I want. I never felt that way with wood. You can look at the clay from different angles and it all makes sense. And you can make sure the bird is balanced. I did a goshawk that wasn't standing right. If I had done it first in clay, that wouldn't have happened.

I've been thinking about going with Floyd Scholz to Cornell. They have a raptor center there. He says I should bring clay and work it while I look at live birds. That would be great. And what's nice about kept falcons is that they'll sit there on a branch. Ducks and gamebirds are too restless.

Scheeler had planned on doing a sharp-shinned hawk taking off from a branch. This clay model uses tongue depressors for the wings. Scheeler pointed out that details and problems could be worked out throughout the bird with clay.

Scheeler did not do detailed sketches of his birds. But he did at least make a side profile. This is a pattern for a flying willet.

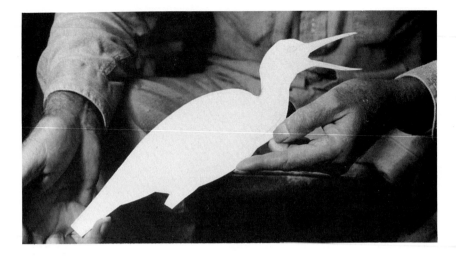

Preferences

A lot of people are doing hawks. They're difficult to do, but different. That's what I've been doing since shortly after I began carving. The majority of my birds have been hawks. The advantage of waterfowl is that you can get all the references you want. You can even buy live birds. But to me, a duck is only pretty in two places, in the water or flying. I don't think they're very good birds standing around. If you see one walk, you'll find it's really clumsy.

I rely on a couple of books for references when I'm doing hawks. One is *Birds of Prey of the World* (by Mary Louise Grossman and John Hamlet), and the other is *A Sketchbook of Birds,* by Charles Tunnicliffe. Tunnicliffe made real accurate drawings from specimens. He would pull feathers out and do paintings of them. The originals were full-size drawings.

I did an Arctic gyrfalcon from a picture and a skin. I never had a specimen. But it worked out pretty well.

I don't think I'll ever do anything as big as a snowy owl. It's pretty big. I like to work on a bird the size of a peregrine or a sharp-shinned hawk. The male sharpie is only ten inches long. But with its wings open, it looks a lot bigger. That's what I've worked up in clay, a sharp-shin taking off from a branch. I do prefer large birds to smaller ones like songbirds. But I've done some shorebirds. They usually have nice colors to them. The willet has beautiful wings, for example.

Basics

Sketches are not much use to me. That's why I'll model a bird in clay and Styrofoam. On a sketch you lose a dimension. But in clay you can see what the total piece will look like. I don't even keep patterns around. I couldn't be a teacher because I don't have a set way of doing things.

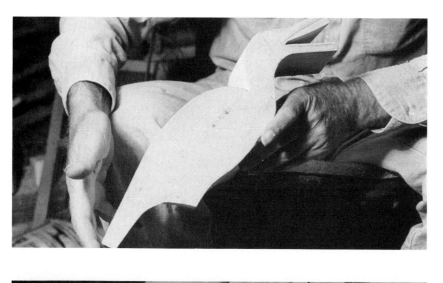

Above left *The wood cutout for the willet.* Above *Scheeler deciding how to turn the head of the bird.* Left *He recommended working from a centerline, which is always the high point on the bird's body.*

I usually start with just a profile of a bird. I might spend the bigger part of a day on that. But when you band saw the wood, it looks as if the pattern grew. Then if you want the head turned, that's a problem. You have to keep adjusting. One of the hardest things to do is to keep the bill straight.

When I get the profile cut, I just take my big cutter and grind on an arc. You get the flow of the bird. And I tell people to start from a high point and work from a centerline. It helps stabilize the rest of the carving.

Flying Birds

Maggioni and McKoy would say that if birds have wings, they belong in the air. But if you're doing a big bird you have a lot of work ahead of you.

With the sharp-shin I'm going to do, the whole piece will be only about eighteen inches high. It will be compact. The emphasis will be on the bird.

I can take aluminum and make the wings for the model. I pound the aluminum and curl it up and then turn it over and pound it again. That way I get the compound curve. Then I'll insert the metal and build up the clay and make a crease line where the scapulars are. The wings will be inserted under the scapular feathers.

This is a cardboard pattern for the wing of the flying sharp-shin. Scheeler demonstrates the double curvature of a wing in flight, across its width and along its length.

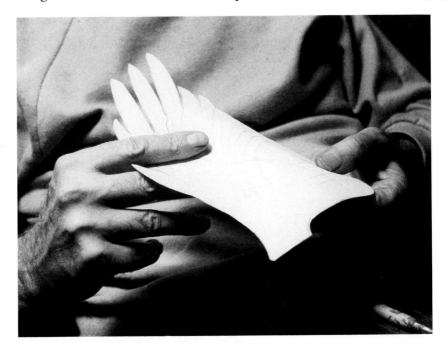

The primaries will have a reverse curve. That's a term I heard from a taxidermist. You need that action to make it a convincing piece. So the primaries won't be tight together, as they would for a gliding bird, like my willet. This sharp-shin will be on the recovery stroke.

The wings will be coming down hard. But you make the reverse curve on only the first three or four primaries. All the strain seems to be on those outer feathers. You can see that on a chukar partridge I did. When a flying bird is done right, it's hard to beat.

With a flying bird it's important to get the stiffness out of the piece. By recreating the stress on the feathers, you can make a bird look convincing. The chukar partridge is just taking off.

Taxidermists have trouble with this movement. They can't seem to get the feather action from the real feathers, though there have been attempts. When a painter tries it, he may fuzz the edges. Bob

Phinney, who does bronzes, puts the reverse curve in his feathers. But he doubles some of the reverse curve to make it look like a quiver. You get the illusion of movement, that the piece is not static.

Wings and Feathers

The first time I used inserts was on a flying black duck. Maggioni persuaded me to do it, though I didn't think I was capable of it. I told him I was too old. But I did a pretty decent job with the bird. I inserted the tail and all the wing feathers. But I made a single slot to insert the primaries and secondaries, plus the upper and lower coverts. I told Maggioni about it and he laughed. He wrote me a letter on how he does it—he makes more than one slot. Why try to put all the feathers into one?

He places the cardboard wing next to the clay model. Scheeler often worked with taxidermy mounts, but he said that the anatomy of a wing in flight could not easily be re-created by taxidermists.

Making feathers is so time-consuming. Back then, I wasn't using a flat slab of wood and steam-bending it for shape: I was carving out every feather. I'd be working until eleven o'clock at night and getting only one or two feathers done. And I was using basswood at the time.

Today if I'm doing inserts, I'll make a pattern for all the major wing feathers, the primaries and secondaries. Then I'll trace my patterns on thin pieces of wood, making sure they're all the same thickness. I use tupelo because you can cut it almost paper thin. Then I'll burn out the feathers rather than use a pair of shears or knife because those tend to split the wood. With burning you seal the edge.

I'll burn my shaft in, and I'll sand the edges from the shaft out to the edge and get it feather thin. I want all the beef in the middle for strength.

Top *To make a wing pattern, Scheeler outlined a real wing on a piece of cardboard. To determine the curvature of the wing, he had only to bend the cardboard and transfer the curve to a thick piece of wood.* Middle *The basic wing of a flying willet shows the curve. This wing is glued temporarily into place so that work can be done on the body and the wing separately or as a unit.* Bottom *This cardboard, a template for laying out the primaries and the secondaries, is placed in the wooden wing of the willet.*

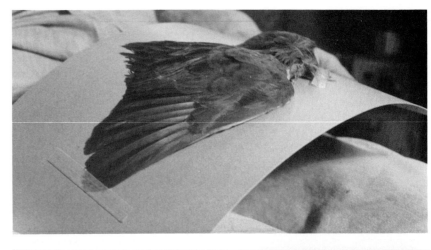

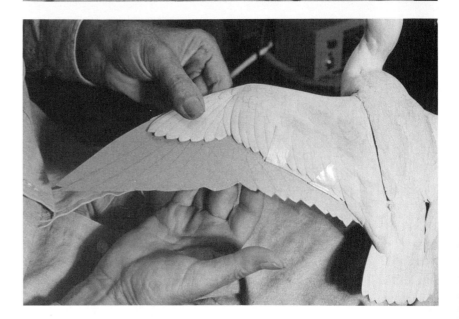

With the burning pen I can shape a feather. I'll burn one side and turn it over and burn the other. The feather will always bend up toward the pen. It will bend up naturally. I'll lay the feather on a board and lift the feather as I'm burning it to give it some shape. But you want every feather to have a common curve so that they lie on top of each other, as real feathers do.

If I want to put a twist in the feather, I use a burning iron with a thin piece of cardboard under it to avoid scorching the wood. Sometimes I'll use hot water and steam to wet a group of feathers. Then I'll press them together on a hard surface and use a hair dryer to dry them. If you do this right you'll get a common bend.

When I burn in the barb lines, I try for about eighty to an inch. On a duck's primaries I would go to about fifty an inch. This burning has made a lot of bad painters into decent painters because of the way burning picks up light. A feather will look just like the real thing provided you have the right shape to it.

When it comes to making the wings, it's hard for me to make a wing and finish it and make the bird and finish it and put the two together. So I rough-carve the body and I'll set the rough-carved wing in under the scapulars. That way there's no seam that shows. Some butt-join wings and camouflage the glue joint, but I don't know what's going to happen to the joint fifteen or twenty years from now. Maybe nothing.

I'll glue a wing temporarily with Hot Melt glue, but it's a strong bond. Then I finish the body and wing together to get the proper fit and take them apart. To do that, I put the bird in the oven and get the temperature hot enough to melt the glue. The wing will fall right off. With tupelo the wood won't check when it dries out in the oven.

Left *Applying heat to one side of a wooden feather allows the carver to bend it so that it looks more natural. When bending a feather with heat, the carver applies a burning tool only to the back.*
Above *A Scheeler feather. Splits and heat allowed Scheeler to have groups of barbs overlap slightly.*

Top right *A clapper rail's wing shows the tight insertion of the primaries and the secondaries as well as the fine burning.* Top left *Not all the wings Scheeler made were inserted with separately made feathers. This bobwhite quail's wing was made from a single piece of tupelo.* Above *The dark lines on the top side indicate that he burned the feather outlines to give them cleaner edges.*

Away from Inserts

On a folded wing, it would be senseless to do individual primaries. You want to keep things consistent looking. That's a bad thing about inserting. It's hard to keep the overall look consistent. It's generally obvious where you inserted a feather. There's what I call a letdown from inserts to where it's not inserted.

Most people do a terrible job with inserts. They're making feathers like tongue depressors, stiff feathers. But Larry Barth did such a fine job with one-piece wings. He got a better transition or flow from the wing structure to the feathers.

The trend is toward solid pieces, but then not many people are making solid birds. Inserts have their place. I would want to insert feathers as a group. I would make but not burn individual feathers and shape them with my burning tool. I'd glue them all together and shave them down to the thickness of one feather and insert that group into the wing slot.

There's too much of a taxidermy look with too much insertion. But take a grouse with its tail fully spread out. When you're getting to the outer feathers, you're going across the grain. So you have to insert groups of tail feathers.

For separating feathers I use a disk that has knife edges. I run up under the feathers to separate them or take a drill and drill through and pull or push it along the length of the feather. I did this on the tail of a broad-wing I did. The tail has twelve feathers but it's in two parts. I got the basic shape from a one-and-a-half-inch-thick block. I remember I attached the tail and then I couldn't get under it to burn.

Unfinished broad-winged hawk, 1986. Above left The wings of this hawk were made as separate pieces. Above right An inserted piece of brass tubing in epoxy accepts a piece of brass imbedded in the wing. Left The hawk's tail, made in two sections.

Details of unfinished broad-winged hawk, 1986.

Composition

My main thing is composition. I put the carving second and the texturing third. For every smooth part of a carving I think you should have a heavily textured area to balance it. You wouldn't want the whole thing smooth or textured.

With color, you want complementary colors just for accent, but not too much. If I see a certain color in the bill, I'll try to get something in the base to complement it. I did a couple of ruddy turnstones. They're reddish. I had things on the base that you find along the beach: shells, sea grass. I also carved a crab pincer from a rock crab that had turned red. For a green heron I did, I used plants that had the same color as the bird.

If it's just a bird on a branch, I like to use a color of a branch that's going to work with the color of my bird. I did that with a thrush. For a merlin, the bark on the pine branch worked with the blue-gray color on the bird. If I was doing a bird that had a lot of blue with some flowers, I'd try to pick a complementary flower, an orange one. That's not saying that a bluebird doesn't land on an apple tree. That would work too. But I have seen some carvings using a blue flower with a bluebird, and that doesn't work.

Bases are getting simpler. They were once like habitat displays. It was something natural history museums did. To me using a lot of habitat is a crutch to get the attention off the bird. Now we try to keep everything simple. With all that habitat, it looked like you were trying to put a little bit of the outdoors into your house. People would make spiders, animals crawling around. I never liked it. There's power in simplicity.

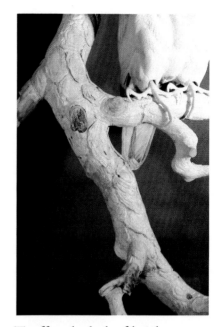

To effect the look of height, Scheeler made this branch descend onto a block of teakwood. Made from tupelo, the branch simulates a pine tree.

Out on a Limb

That's the way I see this goshawk I put on a branch. It's a simple vignette. A portion of a branch hangs down, bypassing the base so you get the illusion that it's hanging. You use your imagination as to whether it's twenty feet up or whatever. The bird seems to be sitting up in a tree. You wouldn't be able to put that branch in the opposite direction, having it come out of the block. It would look like it's growing out of the wood. Painters do this kind of thing all the time. But the problem with a branch is you have only one good view of it. The back side of a branch has nothing. The foliage is on the outside length. The only good view is looking right at it because of the way the foliage grows. But it's still a good way to view a bird. This piece had pine needles. They held the arrangement together. You can fill in spaces with them and have blank spaces. They're mass without weight. That's what Larry Barth says. They're very airy looking. And they're something that can be made easily.

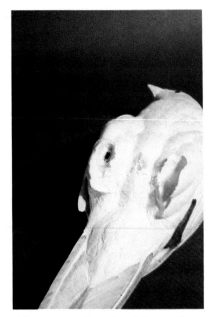

Above *Underside of the unfinished goshawk to be mounted on the branch. On the left is the brass tubing that accepts the foot. Between the feet can be seen the remains of a piece of metal. Scheeler used a length of steel as a temporary connection between bird and branch so that he could move the bird around for the proper stance.* Above right *Prior to mounting the bird, Scheeler made feet out of tupelo. But only one foot supports the bird, as indicated by the steel insert.*

I'm thinking of doing something like this again with a bird flying around the limb. The branch would be a good support. The bird only has to touch it.

When you're using a single bird, it's hard to have much going on for you. With two birds you can make an arrangement. The more birds, the better the arrangement, like a bouquet of flowers. But it's probably better to use an odd number of birds, three rather than two. I try to make my single birds as interesting as I can. I turn a head a little bit or open a mouth or have a tail spread or lift one leg up. Just try to make it interesting and get a good, lively look in the head.

Everything should be subordinate to the bird. That goes for the branch or wood. When I first went to shows, I would hear, Where did you get that beautiful piece of driftwood? They never saw the bird. And that's why I don't like to do songbirds. It's hard to play up the bird and keep the piece compact.

A Green Heron and Pitcher Plants

I think I got a good look on this green heron. It was also the last time I did a base with a lot of habitat. I made these pitcher plants a year before I made the heron. They were so interesting looking. I made, I guess, ten of them. I arranged them in a piece of soft wax, putting the stems in the wax for the design I wanted. But I didn't know what bird I wanted to make with them. About a year later it struck me to do a green heron because it would pick up the same colors that are in the pitcher plants. That's how the composition came about.

The plants I made out of tupelo. It's a tough wood, so you can make thin petals, leaves, and stems with it. Pitcher plants grow in my area. I remember seeing a green heron when I was picking them.

Left *Pitcher plants made from tupelo surround an animated green heron. Scheeler sometimes made a base and decided on the bird later.* Below *Wood shavings that became the moss for the heron's habitat.*

The stones for the composition are a wood putty. But if I did them over again, I would carve them. The moss came from shavings from a Foredom. I used a real coarse cutter. I wet the wood and that's the way it came off. If I had put a router on wet wood, the wood would have come off stringy. Then I made a green stain.

The rest of the base was made out of Durham's Rock Hard Water Putty. It's a powder and you add water to it. But it gets awfully heavy. So I used plastic foam pellets as a base and put the putty over them.

Right *The underside of the heron's wing with inserted feathers.*
Below *Scheeler added extra
feathers to help disguise the connection of wing to body.*

If I had wanted a granular look on the stones, I would have put
a sloppy coat on first, then added powder to the leftover wet mix
and stirred it up. Next I'd have sprinkled the mix over the sloppy
coat, then taken an atomizer with water and sprayed everything,
using a fine mist. That fuses it all together. That's what I did for a
scoter composition.

Left *A close-up of the green her-on's face.* Below *The feet made of tupelo.*

Right *Scheeler often spoke of capturing the attitude or look of a species. These surf scoters have an attentive look. They are also well balanced with rocks of contrasting color and almost equal volume.* Below *The rocks are carved, painted, and sanded.* Below right *Scheeler wanted to portray a sampling of the scoters' habitat, including oyster shells.*

Surf Scoters

For the big rocks of the surf scoters, I just rough-carved them out of basswood and took heavy outdoor latex paint and left the lid off for a while. It took a few days to thicken up. I brushed a heavy coat on the rocks and stippled them. You do that with a brush. You put the paint on and raise it up. Then I sanded the paint down to get the high points off the stipple. I mixed up some thin coats of acrylic stains and washed them over the rocks, which made them gray. To get back the white, I sanded again. But I didn't go down in the crevices. I was just sanding the high spots. Then I made up another coat of acrylic stain and went over everything because I didn't want a bright white. I used sienna or raw umber. I wanted the effect of weathered stone.

I wanted a pretty good contrast between the rocks and the birds. I think that's what makes the piece, which is why I used stones of that color. I think you see stones like that in Maine, the birds' habitat.

The shells are oyster shells. I carved those. When you see some just showing the insides, you find the black mark where the muscle is. That sort of matches the color of the birds. I also picked up colors

One of the scoters. The coloration was achieved with burning lines and Rustoleum paint.

Scheeler wanted a strongly posed bird. The feet, made from wire and epoxy putty.

of the bills in my shells by using thin washes of the same color. It seemed to tie everything together. I even carved an old feather.

I wanted the turned base to look like a piece of driftwood. I scratched it all up, tried to give it a weathered look.

The scoter is a bird many people don't get to see close up. I picked two drakes for the composition. We have three kinds of scoters along the coast. There's the surf scoter, the white-winged scoter, the common scoter. They're all black, but the surf scoter has more white on it than the other two. The scoter is the only truly black duck we have.

Scoters like to sit up on rocks, and if you approach them from a distance, they get that alert look. I wanted that in the carving.

The primary and scapular areas are all inserted. The tail feathers are inserted. Some of the body feathers are laid up like shingles. I burned clear through the wood to get that look.

I won a Best in Show at the U.S. National with them. When I had it at The World, the light was kind of bad. And my birds are dark. The judges brought in someone with a strong light. Well, I didn't make them to be seen under that kind of light. There are a lot of things you wouldn't see otherwise. But I didn't make them to be finely finished.

People don't believe me when I tell them this, but I just used a can of Rustoleum, a spray can. I sprayed the birds with that. I didn't use an undercoat. I went directly to the wood. Carvers claim that black is the hardest color to deal with. What happened, there's a thin coat of black on the birds so that you're seeing some of my burn marks. They're a deep brown. But then I put a gloss coat of varnish over everything to give some life to the color. A clear gloss gave me the effect I wanted. I did the same thing with a crow underneath a goshawk.

A Skinned Crow

With my goshawk and crow composition, I didn't want something competing with the hawk, so I chose a crow. Too much color below the goshawk would have been in conflict with the main subject.

I pulled the skin off a dead crow and had a little body like a chicken on a plate. Doing this I knew exactly where the legs came off the body and where the wings came off. There are no feathers to hide anything. You can get a good accurate pattern. I did that with the surf scoters.

I carved a featherless crow and made the legs separately. Those I positioned. The body feathers I made separately and laid those back to front up to the neck. I had a little extension on each feather. I held my burning iron on each extension and lifted the feather to give me a place to glue it down.

Top *This was the way the carved crow began for what is perhaps Scheeler's most famous composition, a goshawk and dead crow.* Middle *The head was made as a separate piece, and the crow's feathers were made as separate pieces and glued in place.* Bottom *The inserted tail feathers indicate the very fine burning Scheeler was capable of.*

The mantling goshawk with its separate wings, and inserted primary and secondary feathers.

I made a head and carved it like a funnel. I slipped that over the neck feathers and squeezed them down a little bit. It worked out pretty well. That's the only way I could have gotten the effect of the head lying back and the feathers cracked open.

I got a good effect with a starling by using separate feathers. It has these spiky feathers that stand off from each other, which would have been impossible to carve. Someday I'd like to do the same technique on a grouse that's been hit by a goshawk. I'd have it lying on its back with its breast feathers cracked open.

I like the goshawk because he seems to have the fiercest look of them all. And he's a pretty bird. I intend to do all the birds of prey.

A *Clapper Rail*

I still like shorebirds. I did this clapper rail. If you're out on a salt marsh, you'll hear them holler all over the meadow. That's the way I wanted to portray this one. Just making a lot of noise and taking off.

I used a few things you find around their habitat. They live in salt marshes, and you'll find empty oyster shells in there, so that's what I carved.

I wanted him on one foot. I cut a groove along it and put a piece of wire in the groove. It comes out the bottom. Then I got a piece of square tubing in the hobby shop, which I dropped into a hole I made in the habitat. Five-minute epoxy held it in place. I put some grease into the opening in case glue got into it. Before the epoxy set up, I slipped the bird's foot wire into the square brass and moved it around until I got the attitude I wanted. Then I slipped the bird out and let the epoxy set.

For interest, I made the mouth open and inserted the tongue last. I just glued it in.

Left *The clapper rail as Scheeler had seen it, ready to take off.* Above *Carved oyster shells make up the minimal habitat.*

Top *The feet for the rail were made as separate pieces.* Middle *A small piece of square tubing in the base accepts the protruding foot wire.* Bottom *The proper stance.*

Louisiana Herons

I think I've had most of my success with my arrangements because I try to keep things interesting. When I did a pair of Louisiana herons, I could have made them standing up stiff-legged, and they can stand that way, but they wouldn't have looked very nice.

They have almost an Oriental look to them. The Japanese print makers use a lot of herons. My birds have a lot of twisty curves. They have a flow that goes up and comes back. It's continuous. Nothing leads you out or gets you hung up.

All of this came out of my head. I had an idea of what I wanted, although my original thought was to have a long piece of wood with two herons. I just compressed the idea a little, but it still came out of my head.

On a bird a body is a rigid frame. You can't bend the body. So the only things you can change on it are the wings, the legs, the tail, the neck. For the herons, I wanted one body tipped in one attitude, the other in another attitude. Then I figured out how to arrange the legs and necks.

The whole thing is a design piece. It's an S composition. If you follow the bird up from one foot to the neck, it brings you right back to the foot. If you look at the two of them, your eye does the same without going out of the picture. The viewer is zeroed in on the birds. That's why I didn't have any habitat. I didn't want anything disrupting the space around them.

The necks and bodies are one piece, the heads are separate. The wings I made separately and the legs are separate pieces.

One of Scheeler's most interesting designs is a pair of Louisiana herons. He made the most of the long, twisting necks. Interestingly, he did not make models prior to carving the birds.

Above *Scheeler at work on his last carving, a peregrine falcon.* Below *This was a false start. The head pose was not to his liking.*

Bronzes

When I was working for Doug Miller, he wanted to make bronzes of some of my birds. He did make a bronze of my prairie falcon and dove. But it would have been far better if I had made the piece out of clay and done it in such a way that it picked up light differently. You don't go in for detail in bronze the way you do in wood.

When you carve a bird, you do detail. But with a bronze you're looking for a good confirmation of shape. You do it loosely. There's a stage that I like when I'm carving a bird. The bird would look great even if I didn't paint it. Then I have to refine all the stuff, and the bird doesn't look good to me anymore.

So I'd like to do a nice bronze piece sometime, but not a wood carving converted into a bronze. I'd do it in clay first.

The Making of a Peregrine

My favorite falcon is a gyrfalcon. The next would be a peregrine. It's a familiar bird to me, but not everybody sees one. I just like it.

For this bird I started out with a piece of tupelo six by eight by twenty-four inches. I got it from Curt's Waterfowl Corner.

I work on attitude a lot. If I want an alert look, I'll raise the neck up, tighten the feathers down. If I want a rested look, I'll pull the head down and loosen the feathers up on the breast and the scapular areas.

I turned the head to make this peregrine more interesting looking. It was slow going because the head and body were one piece. I don't want the head separate because I don't want to take the chance of a seam showing. When adding a head, you have to get the pose right the first time before you glue it down. So I like to do all this as one piece. But you should have a reference line drawn down the middle of the head. Then you want one across the eyes at right angles to the other line. I'm also careful to leave a brow over the eyes. That helps with the look. I can always flatten it out later.

I carved the bird with its primaries on and then cut them off. I used a grinder to do it. Some people like to make a stop cut, but the problem with that is, if you don't grind down to the bottom of it, you'll have a mark. By cutting the primaries off, I could work on the tail area and tail coverts and get all that burned. Then I made the primaries as a separate group and inserted them. That way I could finish their undersides, burn them and paint them. I couldn't do that on the bird, and you can see that area. In order to be consistent with the rest of the bird, I had to finish under those feathers. But by carving them with the rest of the bird in the first place, I could keep the flow of the bird in perspective and have the primaries in their proper attitude.

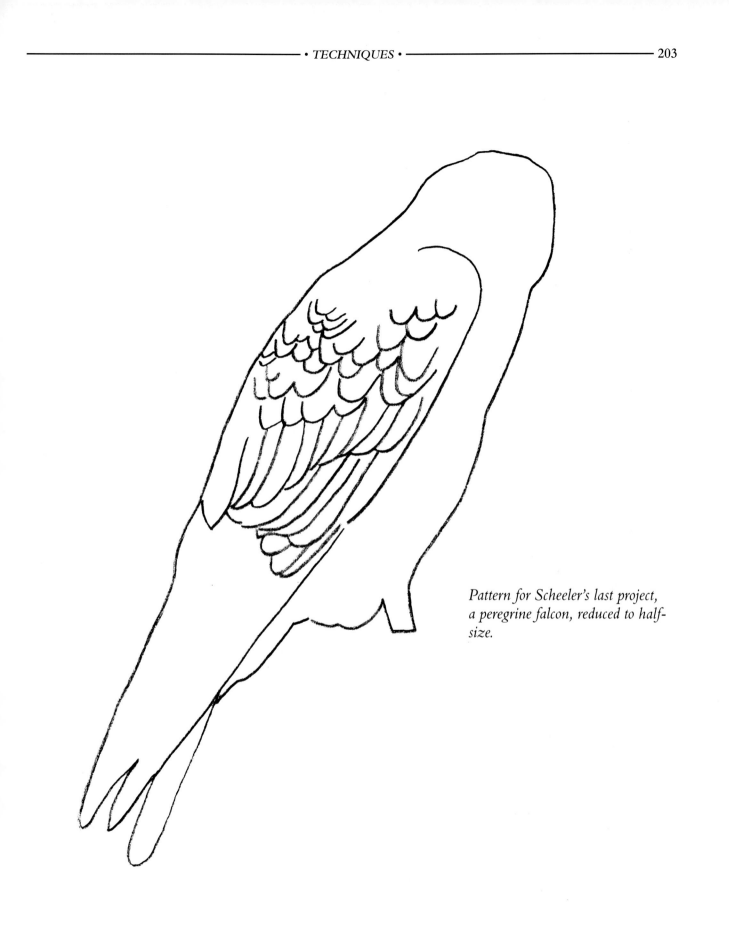

Pattern for Scheeler's last project, a peregrine falcon, reduced to half-size.

Right *This was his second attempt at the peregrine. Scheeler decided that had he made clay models for all his birds, he would not have made these false starts. Had Scheeler continued with this bird, he would have needed to remove another 15 to 20 percent of the wood. Below Scheeler carved the entire bird with its primaries in place. Then, using a grinding bit rather than a knife, he removed the primaries and inserted ones made from separate pieces of wood.*

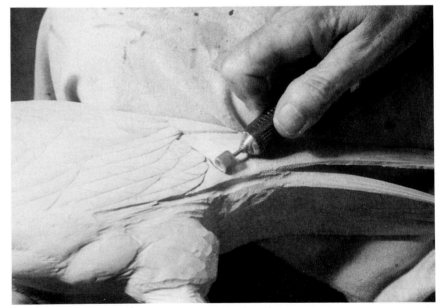

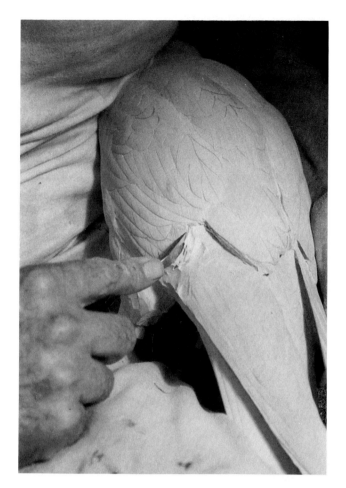

Left *Some cleanup work could be done with a knife, but not too much, since he did not want to cut a line into the wood.* Below *Only by removing the primaries could Scheeler work under that area. He carved the bird with its primaries on to know exactly how they would come off the body.*

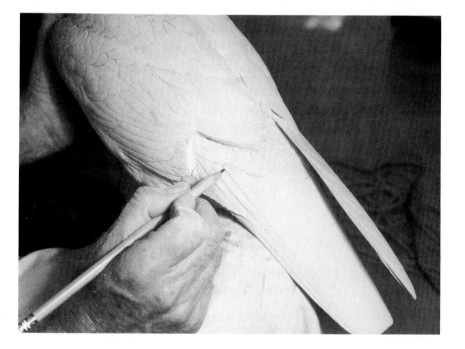

Modeling

I call working on the surface modeling. On the breast, where it's puffed up, you have lumps and bumps. I won't texture individual feathers there. I'll texture in details and along with the paint I can get a loose, puffy look. So I'll use a Gesswein tool with a small, cylindrical stone. I'll lace and weave the feathers together.

On the back, which has the hard feathers, the patterns are pretty symmetrical. But you have to keep the feather groups tight. I draw the feather patterns first on Mylar paper after I do the outline of the wing. I draw the feather patterns within that outline with a soft

Right *A small abrasive stone can put definition around the beak.* Below *Stoning in texturing on the breast. Fluting running in two directions leaves a very smooth surface on the wing.*

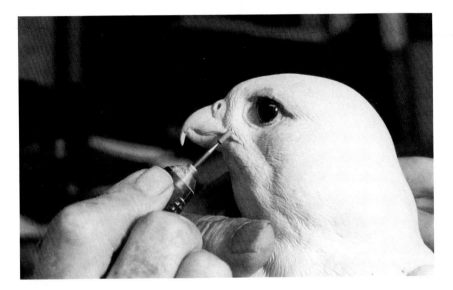

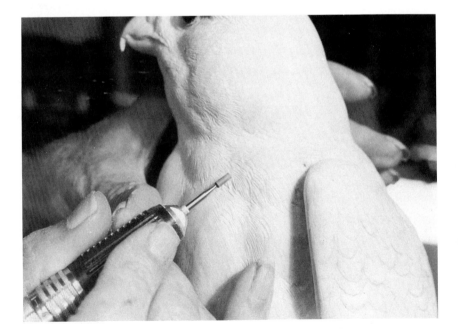

pencil. Then I'll darken the other side with the pencil and lay the Mylar on the wood. This way I can transfer the pattern when I press in the front of the Mylar. I'll do the same thing on the primaries. It's like using a piece of carbon paper.

When cutting, I first relieve each feather, going around its edge. I do this to put shape into each one, like shaping a cluster of grapes. You first get the shape of the cluster and then you can paint or carve each individual grape. I use a cutter with a rounded point. I always lay that flat to the feathers. You don't want them to look too deep. One of the biggest mistakes the novices make is putting gulleys along the edge of each feather. That comes from holding the bit at too much of

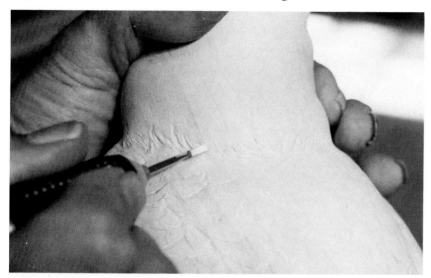

Left Working on the transitional area between what Scheeler described as the soft feathers of the head and the hard ones on the back and wings. *Below* Working with a grinding stone on an area of soft feathers that overlaps a wing.

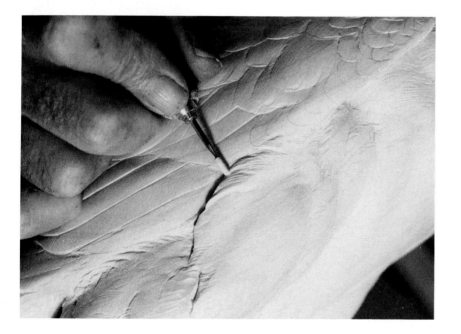

an angle. So I lay it right on the feather. Then I'll make splits on the back feathers with a grinding stone, but not too many.

After that, I'll take a piece of sandpaper and try to soften the hard feather edges left by the bit. A cloth-backed paper is pliable and softens the edges up. I do that about one-third into each feather.

To get out the scratches left by the sanding, I use a piece of coarse steel wool. I make sure to follow the flow of the feathers. That's why I draw in the shafts: so I know in what direction to run the steel wool.

I might have to pencil the shaft lines back in as a guide to burning. And every three fourths of an inch or so I'll draw some guidelines for the barbs. When I burn, I'll do those first and fill in between.

This is the third and final attempt at the peregrine. Note the muscular look on the chest of the bird, a hallmark of Scheeler's birds of prey.

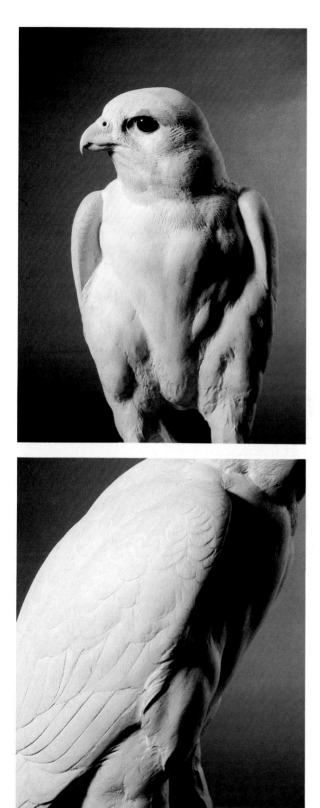

Above left and right *Scheeler saw peregrines as birds with intense, penetrating stares. Note that Scheeler set the eyes in a two-part epoxy putty.* Left *Areas in transition.*

Top *Scheeler worked out feather patterns on a polyester film called Mylar. He would then transfer those patterns to the wood. When you draw on the front of the Mylar and rub the back of it with a soft lead pencil, the Mylar acts like carbon paper.* Middle *Scheeler used a steel cutter that comes from the tool-and-die industry. He recommended holding the cutter as flat as possible so that the feathers would not be raised like shingles.* Bottom *Scheeler also used an offset skew chisel to cut around feathers. With this tool, he avoided cutting down into the wood, which would leave a difficult-to-disguise line.*

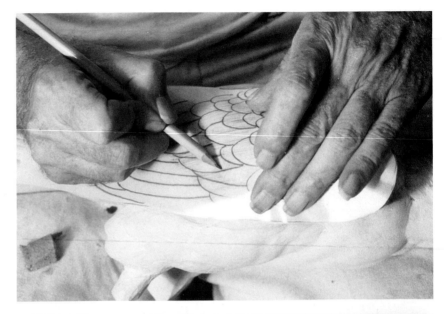

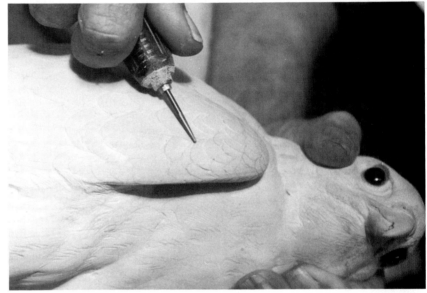

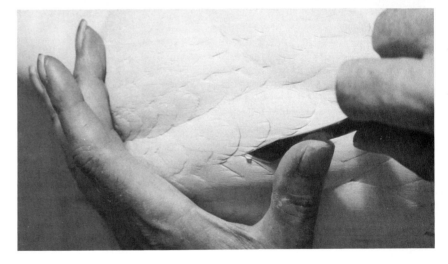

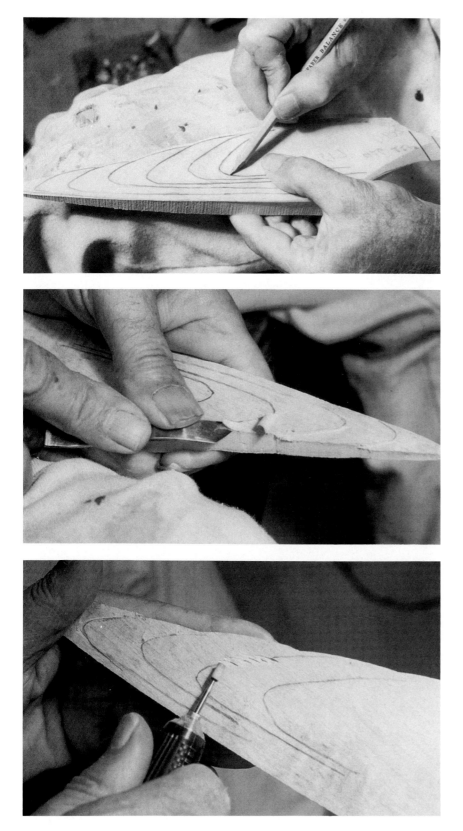

Above *The cut-in feather patterns on the wing.* Top left *For the primaries, Scheeler used Mylar with the individual feathers drawn on it. These could then be transferred to the wood. The feathers were first raised with a grinding stone, which does not leave a sharp line in the wood.* Middle *More wood is removed with the skew chisel.* Bottom *Making splits.*

Right *Sanding the hard feathers from their centers to their edges to give them roundness. Scheeler used a cloth-backed sandpaper for this. Steel wool is used later to remove the marks left by the sandpaper.* Middle and bottom *Laying out some of the barb lines as a guide to burning.*

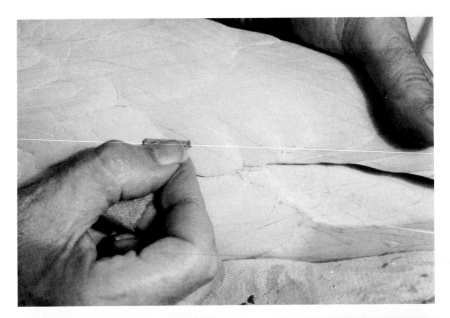

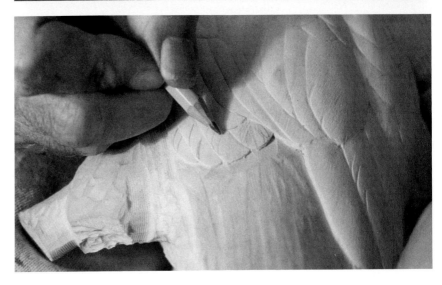

Thoughts on Paints

I painted for a living. I went into business for myself and did mostly commercial work. Most of it was for the telephone company in the area. I learned a little about mixing colors. I do it all by using complementary colors. If I want to gray down a red, I'll go to a green, the opposite on the color wheel. Other carvers would use an umber or a black. I see people who use a lot of umber. The birds get repetitious looking. Someone like Larry Hayden will use umber with other colors and do a super job, but not everyone can do that. The umber dominates.

I've tried acrylics, but I'm used to blending oils. The only advantage to acrylics is that you can handle the bird more. With oils you can't. I have to prop the bird up. But using acrylics is not faster. It's just that they dry faster. You use more steps than oils—washes, washes, over and over. It's not worth it to me. I don't have the patience for acrylics. But the sheen they give is constant—in fact, too much can get plastic looking. You can clean acrylics up with water and you don't have the smell of turpentine. With an oil paint, you don't have that much control. But Marc Schultz solved that by using a formula of driers and turpentine.

Above left *Textured wing.*
Above right *Detail of textured primaries.*

The peregrine with a completely textured breast. Scheeler's original design was to have this bird on a branch, but a goshawk took its place. The peregrine was later perched on a rock.

I don't try to speed up the drying time of my oils. They usually dry overnight. But if you're not used to oils, you can end up with muddy colors pretty easily.

Painting a Peregrine

I sealed this bird with something different, Minwax oil finish. It's a grade of linseed oil. I brushed it on and let it penetrate for five minutes. Then I took a tack cloth and wiped the excess off. Mainly what I used it for was the texturing on the breast. Tupelo gets worn with handling, but the oil penetrates and makes the wood pretty hard, I found. I had trouble getting my gesso to bond to the wood without it.

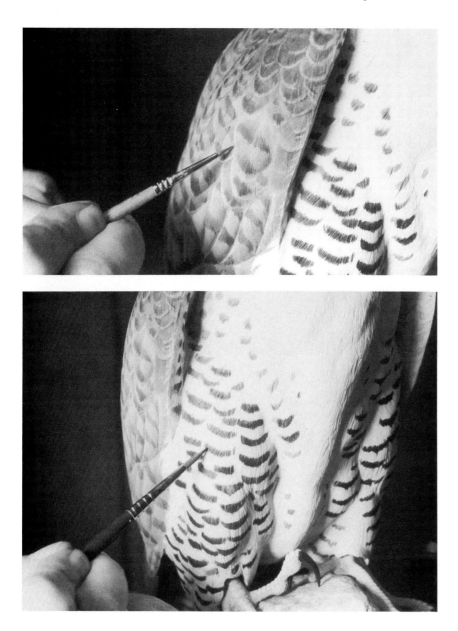

Top left *Putting details on the wings with a Kolinsky sable brush.* Left *Working on the feather patterns. Sable brushes will hold a point.* Above *The painted primaries.*

Then I sprayed a coat of Lok Tite over my oil finish. That, too, is an oil base sealer and dries fast, ten to fifteen minutes. It's a bit flat. I put a thin coat of gesso over that.

I paint with real thin oils. They won't cover the white of the gesso, so I use a base of water color. That dries in five minutes. With burning you have to keep things thin so you don't clog the burn lines. I keep the paints pretty liquid and they dry faster that way.

I mix up 50 percent turpentine, 50 percent kerosene, the fine kerosene used in oil lamps. It has a viscosity to it. Pure turpentine would run down the burn lines. Then I put a couple of drops of cobalt drier in there.

For the back of the peregrine, I made a gray. The breast is white, and I put the black pattern in the head. The grays and blacks are a

Details of the almost finished per-egrine. The rock was carved from a piece of tupelo and placed on a square black base.

mixture of burnt sienna and ultramarine blue with white and a touch of cadmium red light. I can get my blacks down to a light blue with just those three colors. Even the black markings on the breast are the same mixture. The rest of the bird is just white with a little umber.

The Peregrine's Base

I used a block of basswood for the base under the rock. I put automobile primer on it, sanded it all down, and sprayed it with an automobile black, about twelve coats.

The rock is a piece of tupelo, rough-carved so it would look like a rock. I put a heavy coat of gesso on it. I used a sash brush, the kind you paint windows with, and bounced it on the surface. The gesso bonded real good. I used to use Rock Hard Water Putty, but that would come off in sheets, especially on end grain, which sucks the water out. I could have used industrial texture paints or modeling paste, which is much stiffer. Grumbacher and Liquitex make the paste. It's basically gesso with a lot of marble dust in it. Even if I used modeling paste, I would put gesso down first. It bonds the best, and the modeling paste sticks better to gesso than to bare wood.

So I stippled the gesso with a stiff brush and blow-dried it. I rubbed fine sandpaper over it and cleaned it all off. Then I made a real watery wash of black and went over the whole rock. I took sandpaper again and went over the rock lightly. What happens, you're only sanding off the high spots of textured gesso and you have all these white marks and the gray. The black, mixed thin, settles in the crevices. Then I went over the rock with another thin coat of black, which stained the white marks and made the dark a little darker. Then I washed real thin yellow oxide over that, putting some rust stains on the rock. I let it run and blow-dried it.

I used a new paint for the rock. It's called Jo Sonja, made in Australia. A certain percent is acrylic and gouache. It stays pretty flat, and it's resoluble for a while in water. You can't redissolve acrylics. It comes in a two-and-a-half-ounce tube, and all the tubes are pretty much the same price, about $2.50. A tube of acrylic is getting pretty close to $7. Jo Sonja has about forty different tubes. And there's a medium that can control the sheen. I did the feet of the peregrine with this paint. I airbrushed them.

The Art Form

I don't consider a direct copy of something to be good art. But your interpretation is. If you were able to capture a mallard exactly the way it is, it would not be considered good art. I try to capture the personality of the bird with my interpretation.

As for copying someone else's work, I tell people that they can sign my name but they can't sign it the way I do. There is only one John Scheeler.

This bird carving isn't a mechanical thing. If you do it mechanically, you're going to have a mechanical looking bird. So I do it my way, and sometimes I don't even know why I do it that way. When it satisfies me, I stop. That's the way it is with accidental effects. If I'm using a Foredom and grinding away and I get something interesting, I capitalize on that. I play it up.

People call me up and ask how to do something. I'll explain it to them and say it's nothing, just common sense. People are afraid to try things, so they ask. But the top twenty carvers have been willing to experiment rather than look at someone else's carvings.

Maggioni is always talking about not restricting the materials. He used to talk about using plastic and other stuff. Koelpin says that everything should be wood. I look at the end result. Whatever it takes to get an effect, that's all right with me.

When I judge something and it looks good to me, that's what I go by. The measurements may not be right, but what do I know about measurements anyway? I know proportions; I'll know if the secondaries are coming out from the right area.

A profile of the nearly completed piece.

I think the trend today is toward a more sculpted look. But the trend is getting away from being totally anatomically accurate. For example, to show speed you might bring the wings back at a greater angle than is possible, but that gives the feeling of motion. You may have to exaggerate a little.

Grainger McKoy is a master at getting motion. He did these five green-winged teals. They look like they're really moving along. I hope this is where the trend is going, so that what we're doing is accepted as art rather than a direct copy. But you have to be careful not to have the bird look cute or comical. You're still dealing with a wild animal, and you should keep it that way.

Scheeler's Peers

There are some good people in this field. I like Ernie Muehlmatt's style as much as anybody's. He's an artist. He stays close to the real bird, but he knows how to bring the character out, especially with baby birds. Nobody can bring that out the way he can.

When I visited him, I said this isn't a shop, it's a factory. His work area is thirty by forty feet, mine's eight by fourteen. He had stations set up where he grinds and burns and paints. I don't think anybody is as prolific as he is. Maybe Jim Sprankle.

Ernie told me he was going to do a group of birds of some kind for the 1987 World Show. His stuff has such a great feel the way he's doing them. That's probably the way everybody should do birds. He uses what's up in his head so he doesn't spend forever measuring everything. Every time a bird gets in a different position, the measurements change. Proportions are what's important. You'll find out soon enough if a bird's too long or too short.

But someone like Marc Schultz, he does a bird just like a real one. It's like a jewel when he gets done. I don't know how long it takes him to do a bird, but I've never seen burning equal to what he does. He's incredible with burning, changing the amount of burns per inch. He does the finest. And the same with his painting. You'll never see that in my shop. Even if I were capable of fine burning, my patience would run out. New carvers come along and say they want to do their birds like his, and I say that nobody else has ever been able to do it.

I heard he wants to do a hen pheasant. It should be super, especially with a good pose. But generally, you want to be careful you don't end up with the thing looking like a statue, no matter how fine the workmanship.

Larry Barth did a good hen pheasant for the 1981 World. He didn't get anything out of it, but I thought he should have. It was a pretty slick piece. He did a great paint job.

Larry's going to start some blue jays for the 1987 World. He's going to have an inverted pine branch with cones. I tried to talk him out of blue jays. You see them so many times, but he thinks you have to try for a big impact with the judges. He's done some warblers. I think he could win with them. He does great songbirds, and they're real accurate. [Barth finally did take warblers to the World Championships. They finished second.]

Bob Guge is as good as they come. Everything he does is as good as anything I've seen. Whatever he sets his mind to, he'll pull off, even if it's doing a grasshopper. He wants to do juncos. They're not very colorful. They're slate gray all over, but he wants to put them with bittersweet. That's enough accent right there to spark up the composition. Bittersweet has that little shell that opens up. He talks about making some snow with it, but I stay away from that. My snow would look like foam or plastic. Bob likes winter birds. They're subtle.

I'd rate Barton Walter right up there. He did a great blue heron. It's a super piece. Andy Andrews has that and Walter's pair of Canada geese. I think they're the two best pieces in his collection, maybe the two best pieces he'll ever have.

Andy got in touch with me to work for him. I was working for Doug Miller, so nothing I made was available. He wouldn't sell any of it. Andy wanted to know if I needed a change of scenery. I didn't know him from Adam, and Doug was very good to work for. But I agreed to talk to Andy. He asked me what it would take to work for him. I told him how much a year I wanted, but I was careful to make it for five years because if he wanted only a couple of birds, then I'd be back on my own. He went for it.

He wanted to know where I was coming from. He's very loyal and he expects loyalty in return. The first thing he told me was to be candid. I accepted that and I never lied to him. He's been super ever since. And so was Doug.

Scheeler's almost finished peregrine.

PART FOUR

Gallery

Canvasback hen and drake,
Andrews collection

Red-breasted merganser hen and drake, Andrews collection

Kestrel pair, Miller collection

Widgeon pair, Miller collection

Scaled quail, Miller collection

Green-winged teals, Miller collection

Wood duck pair, Miller collection

Black duck, Miller collection

Peregrine and green-winged teal, Miller collection

Goshawk and blue-winged teal, Miller collection

Arctic gyrfalcon and oldsquaw,
Miller collection

Mourning dove, Miller collection

Peregrine falcon, Miller collection

Merlin, Miller collection

Marsh hawk, Miller collection

Bobwhite quail, Miller collection

Roadrunner, Miller collection

American avocet, Miller collection

Virginia rail, Miller collection

*Prairie falcon and mourning dove,
Miller collection*

Long-eared owl and mouse, North American Wildfowl Art Museum

Arctic terns, Miller collection

Harris' hawk and rabbit, Miller collection

Arctic gyrfalcon, Miller collection

Ruffed grouse pair, North American Wildfowl Art Museum

Goshawk and crow, North American Wildfowl Art Museum

Surf scoters, Wildlife World Museum

Following pages:

Kestrel, courtesy of S. Scott Hutchinson

Doves in tandem, Leigh Yawkey Woodson Art Museum

Louisiana herons, Wildlife World Museum

Following pages:

Willet, North American Wildfowl Art Museum. Courtesy of Breakthrough *magazine*

Clapper rail, North American Wildfowl Art Museum. Courtesy of Breakthrough *magazine*

Prairie falcon, Andrews collection

Merlin, Andrews collection

Kestrel, courtesy of S. Scott Hutchinson

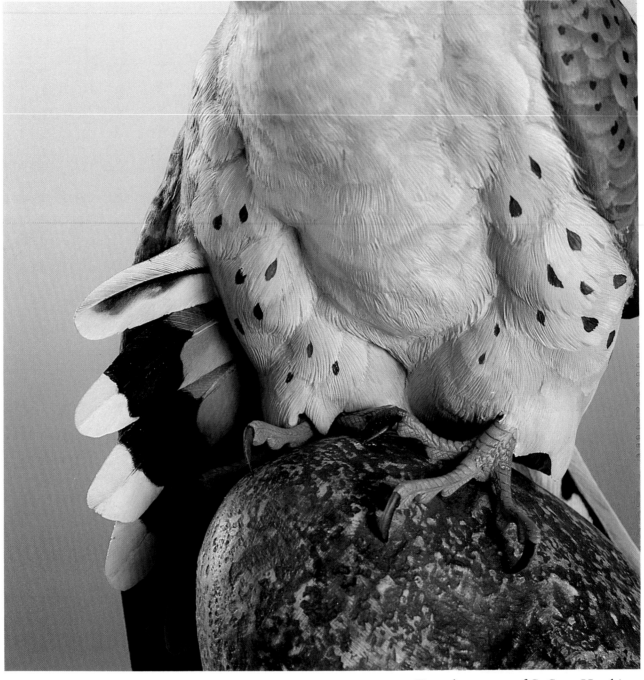

Kestrel, courtesy of S. Scott Hutchinson

Chukar partridge, Andrews collection

Louisiana blue heron, courtesy of
S. Scott Hutchinson

*Sharp-shinned hawk and starling,
Andrews collection*

*Sharp-shinned hawk and starling,
Andrews collection*

Facing page:

*Hermit thrush, Andrews
collection*

Black duck, Andrews collection

Broad-winged hawk, Andrews collection

Peregrine falcon, Andrews collection

Appendix

Bibliography
Magazines of Interest
Other Books by the Author
Competitions and Exhibitions

Bibliography

Alcorn, Gordon Dee. *Owls.* Prentice Hall Press. 1986.

Armstrong, Robert H. *Guide to the Birds of Alaska.* Alaska Northwest Publishing Company. 1983.

Audubon, John James. *The Birds of America.* Crown Publisher. 1966.

Austin, Oliver L., and Singer, Arthur. *Birds of the World.* Golden Press. 1961.

Aymar, Gordon. *Bird Flight.* Dodd, Mead & Company.

Bahrt, Sidney, and Jex, Hope S. *A Wilderness of Birds.* Doubleday & Company.

Barber, Joel. *Wild Fowl Decoys.* Dover Publications. 1954.

Beebe, C. William. *The Bird: Its Form and Function.* Dover Publications. 1965.

Beebe, Frank L. *Hawks, Falcons, & Falconry.* Hancock House Publishers. 1976.

Bellrose, Frank C. *Ducks, Geese and Swans of North America.* Stackpole Books. 1980.

Boag, David, and Alexander, Mike. *The Atlantic Puffin.* Blanford Press. 1986.

Boulton, Rudyerd. *Traveling with the Birds.* M. A. Donahue & Company. 1960.

Boyer, Trevor, and Burton, Philip. *Vanished Eagles.* Dodd, Mead & Company. 1981.

Brown, Leslie, and Amadon, Dean. *Eagles, Hawks & Falcons of the World,* Vols. I and II. Country Life Books. 1968.

Bruce, David. *Bird of Jove.* Ballantine Books. 1971.

Bruun, Bertel, and Zim, Herbert S. *Birds of North America.* Golden Press. 1966.

Burk, Bruce. *Game Bird Carving.* Winchester Press. 1982.

————. *Decorative Decoy Designs, Dabbling and Whistling Ducks.* Winchester Press. 1986.

Burk, Ken, ed. *How to Attract Birds.* Ortho Books. 1983.

Burn, Barbara. *North American Birds,* The National Audubon Society Collection Nature Series. Bonanza Books. 1984.

Burton, John A., ed. *Owls of the World.* E. P. Dutton & Company, Inc. 1973.

Burton, Robert. *Bird Behavior.* Alfred A. Knopf, Inc. 1985.

Cade, Tom J. *The Falcons of the World.* Cornell University Press. 1982.

Campbell, W. D. *Birds of Town and Village.* Country Life Books. 1965.

Campell, Bruce, ed. *The Pictorial Encyclopedia of Birds.* Paul Hamlyn, Ltd. 1967.

Casey, Peter N. *Birds of Canada.* Discovery Books. 1984.

Chinery, Michael, and Pledger, Maurice. *Garden Birds of the World.* Dodd, Mead & Company. 1983.

Clark, Neal. *Eastern Birds of Prey.* Thorndike Press. 1983.

Clement, Roland C. *The Living World of Audubon.* Grosset & Dunlop. 1974.

Coleman, Bruce. *Birds.* Crescent Books. 1978.

Coles, Charles, and Pledger, Maurice. *Game Birds.* Dodd, Mead & Company. 1985.

Colio, Quintina. *American Decoys.* Science Press. 1972.

Craighead, John J. and Frank C. *Hawks, Owls and Wildlife.* Dover Publications, Inc. 1969.

Cruickshank, Allan D. *Cruickshank's Photographs of Birds of America.* Dover Publications, Inc. 1977.

Cruickshank, Allan D. and Helen G. *1001 Questions Answered About Birds.* Dover Publications, Inc. 1976.

Cruickshank, Helen G. *The Nesting Season—The Bird Photographs of Frederick Kent Truslow.* The Viking Press. 1979.

Cusa, Noel. *Tunnicliffe's Birds.* Little, Brown and Company. 1984.

Dalton, Stephen. *Caught in Motion.* Van Nostrand Reinhold. 1982.

Davison, Verne E. *Attracting Birds from the Prairies to the Atlantic.* Thomas Y. Crowell. 1967.

Dennis, John V. *A Complete Guide to Bird Feeding.* Alfred Knopf, Inc. 1976.

Derry, Ramsey. *The Art of Robert Bateman.* The Viking Press. 1981.

Dossenbach, Hans D. *The Family Life of Birds.* McGraw-Hill Book Company. 1971.

Dougall, Robert, and Ede, Basil. *Basil Ede's Birds.* Van Nostrand Reinhold. 1981.

Duval, Paul. *The Art of Glen Loates.* Cerebrus Publishing Company, Ltd. 1977.

Earnest, Adele. *The Art of the Decoy: American Bird Carvings.* Schiffer Publishing, Ltd. 1982.

Eckert, Allan W., and Karalus, Karl F. *The Owls of North America.* Weathervane Books. 1987.

———. *The Wading Birds of North America.* Doubleday & Company. 1981.

Elman, Robert, and Osborne, Walter. *The Atlantic Flyway.* Winchester Press. 1980.

Farrand, John, Jr., ed. *The Audubon Society Master Guide to Birding.* Vols. I, II and III. Alfred A. Knopf, Inc. 1983.

Feduccia, Alan. *The Age of Birds.* Harvard University Press. 1980.

Fisher, James, and Peterson, Roger Tory. *World of Birds,* rev. Crown Publishers. 1969.

Forbush, Edward H., and May, John R. *A Natural History of American Birds of Eastern and Central North America.* Bramhall House. 1955.

Gillette, John, and Mohrhardt, David. *Coat Pocket Bird Book.* Two Peninsula Press. 1984.

Gilley, Wendell H. *The Art of Bird Carving.* Hillcrest Publishers, Inc. 1972.

Gilliard, Thomas E. *Living Birds of the World.* Doubleday & Company. 1958.

Gillmor, Robert. *C. F. Tunnicliffe Sketches of Bird Life.* Watson-Guptill Publications. 1981.

Godfrey, W. Earl. *The Birds of Canada.* National Museums of Canada. 1966.

Godin, Patrick. *Championship Waterfowl Patterns. Book I Puddle Ducks,* 1986. *Book II Diving Ducks,* 1987. Published and distributed by the author.

Gooders, John. *Collins British Birds.* William Collins Sons & Co. Ltd. 1982.

Gooders, John, and Boyd, Trevor. *Ducks of North America and the Northern Hemisphere.* Facts on File Publications. 1986.

Greenway, James C., Jr. *Extinct and Vanishing Birds of the World.* Dover Publications, Inc.

Grossman, Mary Louise, and Hamlet, John. *Birds of Prey of the World.* Clarkson N. Potter. 1964.

Gullion, Gordon. *Grouse of the North Shore.* Willow Creek Press. 1984.

Halliday, Jack. *Vanishing Birds.* Holt, Rinehart and Winston. 1978.

Ham, John, and Mohrhardt, David. *Kitchen Table Bird Book.* Two Peninsula Press. 1984.

Hammond, Nicholas. *Twentieth Century Wildlife Artists.* The Overlook Press. 1986.

Harrison, Colin. *A Field Guide to the Nests, Eggs and Nestlings of North American Birds.* Collins. 1978.

Harrison, George H. *The Backyard Bird Watcher.* Simon and Schuster. 1979.

Harrison, Hal H. *Wood Warblers' World.* Simon and Schuster. 1984.

Heinroth, Oskar and Katharina. *The Birds.* University of Michigan Press. 1958.

Hickey, Joseph J. *A Guide to Bird Watching.* Dover Publications. 1975.

Hickman, Mae, and Guy, Maxine. *Care of the Wild Feathered and Furred.* Michael Kesund Publishing. 1973.

Hosking, Eric. *Eric Hosking's Waders.* Pelham Books, Ltd. 1983.

Hosking, Eric, and Flegg, Jim. *Eric Hosking's Owls.* Pelham Books, Ltd. 1983.

Hosking, Eric, and Lockley, Ronald M. *Seabirds of the World.* Facts on File Publications. 1983.

Hosking, Eric, and MacDonnell, Kevin. *Eric Hosking's Birds.* Pelham Books, Ltd. 1979.

Hummel, Monte. *Arctic Wildlife.* Chartwell Books, Inc. 1984.

James, Ross. *Glen Loates Birds of North America.* Prentice Hall of Canada. 1979.

Jeklin, Isidor, and Waite, Donald E. *The Art of Photographing North American Birds.* Whitecap Books. 1984.

Johnsgard, Paul A. *The Plovers, Sandpipers, and Snipes of the World.* University of Nebraska Press. 1981.

————. *Grouse and Quails of North America.* University of Nebraska Press. 1973.

————. *North American Game Birds of Upland and Shoreline.* University of Nebraska Press. 1975.

Kangas, Gene and Linda. *Decoys A North American Survey.* Hillcrest Publications, Inc. 1983.

Kastner, Joseph. *A World of Watchers.* Alfred A. Knopf, Inc. 1986.

Kress, Stephen W. *The Audubon Society Handbook for Birders.* Charles Scribner's Sons. 1981.

Lacey, John L., and McBride, Tom Moore. *The Audubon Book of Bird Carving.* McGraw-Hill Book Company, Inc. 1951.

Landsdowne, J. Fenwick. *Birds of the West Coast.* Houghton Mifflin Company. 1976.

————. *Birds of the West Coast,* Vol. II. Houghton Mifflin Company. 1980.

Landsdowne, J. Fenwick, and Livingston, John A. *Birds of the Eastern Forest.* Houghton Mifflin Company. 1968.

————. *Birds of the Eastern Forest,* Vol. II. Houghton Mifflin Company. 1970.

————. *Birds of the Northern Forest.* Houghton Mifflin Company. 1966.

Lank, David M. *From the Wild.* North Word, Inc. 1987.

Lawson, Glenn. *The Story of Lem Ward.* Schiffer Publishing, Ltd. 1984.

Laycock, George. *The Birdwatcher's Bible.* Doubleday & Co., Inc. 1976.

LeMaster, Richard. *Wildlife in Wood.* Contemporary Books, Inc. 1985.

Leopold, Aldo. *A Sand County Almanac.* Oxford University Press. 1968.

Line, Les. *Audubon Society Book of Wild Birds.* Harry N. Abrams. 1976.

Line, Les, Garrett, Kimball L., and Kaufman, Kenn. *The Audubon Society Book of Water Birds.* Harry N. Abrams, Inc. 1987.

Lofgren, Lars. *Ocean Birds.* Crescent Books. 1984.

Lyttle, Richard B. *Birds of North America.* Gallery Books. 1983.

Mace, Alice E., ed. *The Birds Around Us.* Ortho Books. 1986.

Mackey, William F., Jr. *American Bird Decoys.* Schiffer Publishing, Ltd. 1965.

Mansell, William, and Low, Gary. *North American Birds of Prey.* William Morrow and Company. 1980.

————. *North American Marsh Birds.* Harper & Row. 1983.

Marcham, Frederick George, ed. *Louis Agassiz Fuertes & the Singular Beauty of Birds.* Harper & Row Publishers. 1971.

Martin, Brian P. *World Birds.* Guinness Books. 1987.

Matthiessen, Peter. *The Shore Birds of North America.* The Viking Press. 1967.

McKenny, Margaret. *Birds in the Garden.* The University of Minnesota Press. 1939.

Merkt, Dixon M. *Shang.* Hillcrest Publications, Inc. 1984.

Mitchell, Alan. *Lambart's Birds of Shore and Estuary.* Charles Scribner's Sons. 1979.

————. *Field Guide to Birds of North America.* National Geographic Society. 1983.

————. *Stalking Birds with Color Camera.* National Geographic Society. 1961.

————. *Water, Prey and Game Birds.* National Geographic Society. 1965.

Mohrhardt, David. *Bird Reference Drawings.* Publication of David Mohrhardt, 314 N. Bluff, Berrien Springs, MI 49103. 1985.

————. *Bird Studies.* Publication of David Mohrhardt, 314 N. Bluff, Berrien Springs, MI 49103. 1986.

————. *Selected Bird Drawings.* Publication of David Mohrhardt, 314 N. Bluff, Berrien Springs, MI 49103. 1987.

Nice, Margaret Morse. *Studies in the Life History of the Song Sparrow.* Dover. 1937.

Patent, Dorothy Hinshaw. *Where the Bald Eagles Gather.* Clarion Books. 1984.

Pearson, T. Gilbert, ed. *Birds of America.* Garden City Publishing Company, Inc. 1936.

Peck, Robert McCracken. *A Celebration of Birds.* Walker and Company. 1982.

Perrins, Christopher, and Middleton, Alex, eds. *The Encyclopedia of Birds.* Facts on File Publications. 1985.

Perrins, Christopher. *Bird Life—An Introduction to the World of Birds.* Peerage Books. 1976.

————. *Birds—Their Life, Their Ways, Their World.* Harry N. Abrams. 1976.

Peterson, Roger Tory. *A Field Guide to the Birds.* Houghton Mifflin Company. 1980.

————. *A Field Guide to Western Birds.* Houghton Mifflin Company. 1961.

Phillips, John C. *A Natural History of Ducks,* Vols. I–IV. Dover.

Poole, Robert M., ed. *The Wonder of Birds.* National Geographic Society. 1983.

Porter, Eliot. *Birds of North America: A Personal Selection.* A&W Visual Library.

Pough, Richard H. *Audubon Water Bird Guide.* Doubleday & Company. 1951.

Ratcliffe, Derek. *The Peregrine Falcon.* Buteo Books. 1980.

Rayfield, Susan. *Wildlife Painting Techniques of the Modern Masters.* Watson-Guptill Publications. 1985.

Reilly, Edgar M. *The Audubon Illustrated Handbook of American Birds.* McGraw-Hill Book Company. 1968.

Rieger, George, and Garrett, Kenneth. *Floaters and Stick-Ups.* David R. Godine Publisher. 1986.

Roedelberger, Franz A., and Groschoff, Vera I. *The Wonders of Wildlife.* The Viking Press. 1963.

Savage, Candace. *Eagles of North America.* North Word, Inc. 1987.

Schroeder, Roger. *How to Carve Wildfowl.* Stackpole Books. 1984.

————. *How to Carve Wildfowl Book 2.* Stackpole Books. 1986.

Schroeder, Roger, and Guge, Robert. *Carving Miniature Wildfowl with Robert Guge.* Stackpole Books. 1988.

Schroeder, Roger, and Muehlmatt, Ernest. *Songbird Carving with Ernest Muehlmatt.* Stackpole Books. 1987.

Schroeder, Roger, and Sprankle, James D. *Waterfowl Carving with J. D. Sprankle.* Stackpole Books. 1985.

Scott, Peter. *Key to the Wildfowl of the World.* Wildfowl Trust. 1957.

————. *Observations of Wildfowl.* Cornell University Press. 1980.

Scott, Shirley L., ed. *Field Guide to the Birds of North America.* National Geographic Society. 1983.

————. *Stalking Birds with Color Camera.* National Geographic Society. 1961.

Shetler, Stanwyn G. *Portraits of Nature Paintings by Robert Bateman.* Smithsonian Institution Press. 1987.

Shortt, Michael Terence. *Wild Birds of the Americas.* Pagurian Press Limited. 1977.

Simon, Hilda. *The Splendor of Iridescence.* Dodd, Mead & Company. 1971.

Small, Anne. *Masters of Decorative Bird Carving.* Winchester Press. 1981.

Snow, David, Chisholm, A. H., and Soper, M. F. *Raymond Ching The Bird Paintings.* William Collins & Company, Limited. 1978.

Spaulding, Edward S. *Quails.* MacMillan.

Sprankle, Jim. *Waterfowl Patterns and Painting.* Greenwing Enterprises. 1986.

Starr, George Ross, Jr. *How to Make Working Decoys.* Winchester Press. 1978.

Stefferud, Alfred, ed. *Birds in Our Lives.* Arco Publishing Company, Inc. 1970.

Stepanek, O. *Birds of Heath and Marshland.* West Book House. 1962.

Stokes, Donald W. *A Guide to the Behavior of Common Birds.* Little, Brown and Co. 1979.

Stokes, Ted, and Shackleton, Keith. *Birds of the Atlantic Ocean.* The Macmillan Company. 1968.

Sutton, George Miksch. *Portraits of Mexican Birds.* University of Oklahoma Press. 1975.

Terres, John K. *The Audubon Society Encyclopedia of North American Birds.* Alfred A. Knopf, Inc. 1980.

———. *Songbirds in Your Garden.* Hawthorn Books. 1977.

Tunnicliffe, Charles. *A Sketchbook of Birds.* Holt, Rinehart and Winston. 1979.

Tyrrell, Robert. *Hummingbirds: Their Life and Behavior.* Crown Publishers. 1985.

Van Wormer, Joe. *The World of the Swan.* J. B. Lippincott Company. 1972.

Waingrow, Jeff, and Palmer, Carleton. *American Wildfowl Decoys.* E. P. Dutton. 1985.

Walsh, Harry M. *The Outlaw Gunner.* Tidewater Publishers. 1971.

Warner, Glen. *Glen Loates A Brush With Life.* Harry N. Abrams, Inc. 1984.

Welty, Joel Carl. *The Life of Birds.* W. B. Saunders. 1975.

Wetmore, Alexander, ed. *Song and Garden Birds of North America.* National Geographic Society. 1964.

———. *Water, Prey, and Game Birds of North America.* National Geographic Society. 1965.

Williams, Winston. *Florida's Fabulous Birds.* World Wide Publications. 1986.

———. *Florida's Fabulous Waterbirds.* World Wide Publications. 1987.

Zeleny, Lawrence. *The Bluebird.* Indiana University Press. 1976.

Zim, Herbert, and Sprunt, Alexander. *Game Birds.* Western. 1961.

Magazines of Interest to Wildfowl Carvers

American Birds, 950 Third Avenue, New York, NY 10022.

Birder's World, 720 E. Eighth St., Holland, MI 49423.

Birding, American Birding Association, Inc., P. O. Box 4335, Austin, TX 78765.

Bird Watcher's Digest. P. O. Box 110, Marietta, OH 45750.

Breakthrough Magazine, P. O. Box 1320, Loganville, GA 30249.

Chip Chats, National Woodcarver's Association, 7424 Miami Ave., Cincinnati, OH 45243.

Continental Birdlife, P. O. Box 43294, Tucson, AZ 85733.

WildBird, P. O. Box 6040, Mission Viejo, CA 92690.

Wildfowl Art, Ward Foundation, 655 S. Salisbury Blvd., Salisbury, MD 21801.

Wildlife Art News, 11090 173rd Ave. N.W., Elk River, MN 55330.

Sporting Classics, 420 E. Genesee Street, Syracuse, NY 13202.

Wildfowl Carving and Collecting, P. O. Box 1831, Harrisburg, PA 17105.

The Living Bird Quarterly, Laboratory of Ornithology at Cornell University, 159 Sapsucker Woods Rd., Ithaca, NY 14850.

Other Books by the Author

How to Carve Wildfowl

How to Carve Wildfowl Book 2

Waterfowl Carving with J.D. Sprankle

Songbird Carving with Ernest Muehlmatt

Carving Miniature Wildfowl with Robert Guge

Woodcarving Illustrated

Woodcarving Illustrated Book 2

A Sampling of Competitions and Exhibitions

This list was compiled from *Wildfowl Carving and Collecting* magazine.

The California Open and Wildfowl Arts Festival
4351 Whittle Ave.
Oakland, CA 94602
Held in mid-February, the show attracts 400 carvers and exhibitors and 8,000 visitors.

Canadian National Decoy Carvers Competition
Sportsmans Association
61 Edgehill Rd.
Islington, Ontario M9A 4N1
This show is held in mid-March with some 300 entries of wildfowl carvings.

New England Woodcarvers Festival and
   Competition
Valley Shore Waterfowlers
43 Ridgeview Circle
Guilford, CT 06437
Held in late October or early November, the show made its debut in 1985.

U.S. National Decoy Show
5 Flint Rd.
Amity Harbor, NY 11701
Held in middle to late March, it is the oldest show of its kind in this country.

Clayton Duck Decoy and Wildlife Art Show
P. O. Box 292
Clayton, NY 13624
Held in July, this show offers auctions, demonstrations, painting, and carving contests.

Loyalhanna Wildlife Art Festival
Loyalhanna Watershed Assoc.
P. O. Box 561
Ligonier, PA 15658
Demonstrations, wildlife films, and an auction are featured in this September show.

Pennsylvania Wildlife Art Festival
R.D. #1
P. O. Box 128A
Glen Rock, PA 17327
This show is held in York in mid-November and features a wide variety of decorative carvings.

Annapolis Wildfowl Carving and Art Exhibition
1144 Riverboat Court
Annapolis, MD 21401
Carving and art exhibits are displayed in this late-January show.

World Championship Wildfowl Carving
  Competition
The Ward Foundation
655 S. Salisbury Blvd.
Salisbury, MD 21801
Held in Ocean City, Maryland, in late April, this show features some 800 carvers and attracts around 16,000 visitors. A three-day show, it is a must for anyone interested in bird carving.

The Ward Foundation Wildfowl Carving and
  Art Exhibition
The Ward Foundation
P. O. Box 703
Salisbury, MD 21801
This early-October show, held in Salisbury, is not a competition but an exhibition of carvings and paintings. Some 150 artists and 9,000 visitors attend.

Louisiana Wildfowl Festival
3112 Octavia St.
New Orleans, LA 70125
Held in New Orleans, this September show features some 300 carvers and exhibitors and about 10,000 visitors.

Leigh Yawkey Woodson Art Museum
    "Birds in Art" Exhibition
Leigh Yawkey Woodson Art Museum
Franklin and Twelfth Sts.
Wausau, WI 54401
This show may come the closest to treating bird sculpture as an art form. It is held from mid-September to early November.

Easton Waterfowl Festival
P. O. Box 929
Easton, MD 21654
This is an early-November, townwide wildfowl art exhibition, featuring 450 carvers and exhibitors and attracting some 25,000 visitors. A number of the carvers in this book and in How to Carve Wildfowl *(Stackpole Books, 1984) exhibit their work there.*

International Decoy Contest
Decoy Contest
P. O. Box 406
Davenport, IA 52805
This is an early-August show that attracts over 100 carvers and some 5,000 visitors.

North American Wildfowl Carving
    Championship
4510 Kircaldy Rd.
Bloomfield Hills, MI 48013
Point Mouille State Game Area is the site for this key show in late September, which attracts nearly 300 carvers.

Cajun Hunters Festival
Rt. 2
P. O. Box 337
Cut Off, LA 70345
Held in the Bayou Centroplex in Galliano, this show features over 100 carvers and exhibitors with some 5,000 visitors.

John Scheeler • Bird Carver

Text design by Tracy Patterson
Composed by Duncanphototype
in Bem with display lines in
Bem Bold, italic and roman
Printed by Arcata Graphics/Kingsport
on 70 lb. Sterling Litho